SURPRISING
MARY

SURPRISING MARY

Meditations and Prayers on the Mother of Jesus

MITCH FINLEY

Resurrection Press
Mineola · New York

Other books by Mitch Finley:

Building Christian Families (with Kathy Finley; Thomas More Publications)

Catholic Spiritual Classics (Sheed & Ward)

Your Family in Focus: Appreciating What You Have, Making It Even Better (Ave Maria Press)

Everybody Has a Guardian Angel... And Other Lasting Lessons I Learned in Catholic Schools (Crossroad Publishing Co.)

Heavenly Helpers: St. Anthony and St. Jude (Crossroad Publishing Co.)

Catholic Is Wonderful (Resurrection Press)

Whispers of Love: Encounters with Deceased Relatives and Friends (Crossroad Publishing Co.)

Season of Promises (Resurrection Press)

Season of New Beginnings (Resurrection Press)

The Joy of Being Catholic (Crossroad Publishing Co.)

The Seekers Guide to Being Catholic (Loyola Press)

First published in March, 1997 by Resurrection Press, Ltd.
P.O. Box 248
Williston Park, NY 11596

ISBN 1-878718-37-1
Library of Congress Catalog Card Number 96-72287

All Bible quotations are from the New Revised Standard Version Bible: Catholic Edition, Copyright 1989, 1993, Division of Christian Education of the National Council of the Churches of Christ in the United States of America.

Cover design by John Murello

Printed in the United States of America.

Contents

Part II
MARY IN THE LITURGY

Part III
MARIAN APPARITIONS

Part IV
MARIAN PRAYERS

Introduction

Veneration of Mary, the mother of Jesus, goes back to the early Christian communities. Affection for and dedication to Mary remained a part of all that was best in Christianity even into the lives of the original Protestant reformers. As Timothy G. McCarthy points out in *The Catholic Tradition Before and After Vatican II* (Loyola Press, 1994), in the sixteenth century Martin Luther and Ulrich Zwingli always observed and preached on the Marian feast days. "Both accepted Mary's virginal conception and perpetual virginity as well as her immaculate conception and total sinlessness." They held up Mary as a superior model of faith, humility, and Christian piety.

Lutheran pastor, Dr. Charles Dickson, confirms this insight. In *A Protestant Pastor Looks at Mary* (Our Sunday Visitor Books, 1996), Dr. Dickson writes:

> Mariology was certainly not a side issue with the reformers. Luther referred to Mary as "the workshop of God," and believed that praise for her should not be based on the qualities of Mary herself but on the grace granted to her. Zwingli defended the use of the Ave Maria as a means of praise to Mary stating, "The more honor and love for Christ, the more also the esteem and honor for Mary." Calvin warned of honoring her as a

person rather than as the selected instrument of God but affirms, "We cannot celebrate the blessings given us in Christ without commemorating at the same time how high an honor God has granted to Mary when He chose to make her the Mother of His only Son."

For various reasons, some perfectly understandable, subsequent centuries of Protestant history abandoned this ancient devotion to Mary. All the same, Catholic, Orthodox and, to a lesser degree, Anglican/Episcopalian Christians maintain to this day the ancient veneration of Mary. It is the purpose of this small book to encourage, nourish, and cultivate that veneration.

The author numbers himself among those who value and celebrate the veneration of Mary while objecting to those who charge that Catholics "worship" Mary. Catholicism insists that God alone deserves worship. Mary, unique among all the saints as the mother of Jesus, is a special guide, example, and companion on the way. At the same time, the author numbers himself among those who are not comfortable with some forms of Marian devotion, in particular more sentimental devotions left over from the 1950s.

This collection of meditations and prayers attempts to spank new life into the idea of friendship with Mary and devotion to her. The Mary you will find in this book is the human Mary and Queen of Heaven who became the mother of God's own Son. This Mary knows how to smile, and she has a sense of humor. This Mary is both strong and merciful. The Mary in this book is no stranger to what the New Testament says about her. The Mary of these reflections is a model of faith for everyone. She is our Blessed Mother who stands with us and leads us to the Lord Jesus, her son, and she would have it no other way.

This is a book for those whose devotion to Mary has been strong and consistent over a lifetime. But it is also a book for those rediscovering Mary, rediscovering the value of devotion to her.

Welcome to this small book of meditations and prayers on Mary, the mother of Jesus and our mother, too. As you will see, it has four sections — Mary in Scripture, Mary in the Liturgy, Marian Apparitions, and a fourth section which includes devotional prayers to Mary both ancient and modern. By fashioning this book along such lines the author hopes to remain united to what is best in Catholicism when it comes to Mary. Scripture is our ultimate resource for devotion to Mary, and the Liturgy is at the heart of our life as a Catholic people. Finally, reflections based on Marian apparitions are limited to those officially approved by the church.

The book you hold in your hands attempts, above all, to be truthful and honest about Mary. The author would like to think that this is a book Mary herself would appreciate.

Feast of Our Lady of the Rosary
October 7, 1996

MARY IN SCRIPTURE

Mary, Mother of the Son of God

But when the fullness of time had come, God sent his Son, born of a woman.... (Galatians 4:4)

Let there be a symphony. Let there be a symphony that starts out quietly, peacefully, slowly, like the rising of the sun on a summer morning; like the rising of the sun over a lush green forest on a summer morning. "God sent his Son." When "the fullness of time had come" God sent not a celebrity or a military hero, but "his Son." Let there be a symphony, and after the opening movement, the quiet movement, let there be a second movement, a powerful movement, a movement that swells with "the fullness of time."

Time is full, like a woman great with child. Time will give birth, that must be it. If "the fullness of time" has come, it *must* be time that will give birth. The Son of God will come into the world in a spectacular way. The sky will open, thunder will crack, an earthquake will make the mountains rise and fall apart. The Son of God will descend on a cloud, and all the peoples of the earth will fall, whomp, on their faces in worship, or faint dead away from the sheer spectacular glory of it all. Can't argue with an event like this. Only a divine being would arrive in such a fashion.

But no. When "God sent his Son" in the "fullness of time," it was not time that gave birth, not time but a woman. Talk about a mind-blowing event. The Creator of the universe decides that "his Son" will be "born of a woman." If that doesn't take the cake and the frosting, too. The Son of God is also the son of a human woman. Fully human, fully divine, he slips into the world in the usual way. Does this shock us? Does this scandalize us? It did not shock or scandalize the Creator of the universe, who thought it was a good idea, so let us keep quiet.

The Son of God looks like an ordinary baby, gurgles, coos, and cries like an ordinary baby, sucks sweet milk from the fullness of his mother's breasts. The first time that ordinary looking baby smiled, well, well . . . his mother felt a touch of heaven's joy like mothers do.

The earliest mention of Mary in the New Testament doesn't even use her name. She is simply "a woman" the Son of God is "born of." Why, do you suppose, that this is so? Was it not important to St. Paul and to the early church to mention Mary's name? Did it not matter who the woman was who gave birth to Jesus? Was Paul just a calculating intellectual who had no feelings for Mary, the mother of Jesus?

On the contrary. Notice, he doesn't use Jesus' name, either. It's as if Paul wanted to whisper in his readers' ears. Come over here, Paul whispers to the Galatians. Here is the most amazing bit of news. Are you ready? Maybe you had better sit down. Here it is: The Son of God — and we all know who I'm talking about — came into the world in the usual way, as all babies do. That's right. His mother was not a spiritual being of some sort. His mother was not an angel. No. The mother of the Son of God — and we all know who I'm talking about — was, get this, a *woman*. An ordinary woman. Yes. As ordinary as she could be. You could pass Mary on the street and not bat an eyelash. She looked like a thousand other young Palestinian women. The ways of God are mysterious.

Of course, St. Paul was saying, we all know who I'm talking about. We all revere Mary, the mother of the Lord Jesus. We all know who I'm talking about. But, Paul was saying, don't forget that she was a woman like countless other women. Now listen, Paul continues. Look. I emphasize the humanity of Mary, I call her simply "a woman" in order to remind you that her son, the Son of God, was just as human as she was. Yes. Jesus was just as human as his mother, just as human as you and I. The Son of God was also fully the son of Mary. He did not arrive on a cloud, he slipped into the world in the usual way, "born of a woman," his belly-button winking at the moon. Therefore, oh yes, "blessed are you among women," Mary. Blessed are you . . . and, by golly, blessed are *we*. Imagine that. Blessed are *we*.

Holy Mary, pray for us that we may grow closer to Jesus. Amen.

No More "Magic Mary"

Then his mother and his brothers came; and standing outside, they sent to him and called him. A crowd was sitting around him; and they said to him, "Your mother and your brothers and sisters are outside, asking for you." And he replied, "Who are my mother and my brothers?" And looking at those who sat around him, he said, "Here are my mother and my brothers! Whoever does the will of God is my brother and sister and mother." (Mark 3:31–35)

Here is Jesus, doing his thing. Here is Jesus, teaching people, shedding some light, sharing some insights. Jesus is a young man on a roll. Suddenly, oh bother, who shows up but his family. To a young man on a roll his family can be a drag. Put yourself in Jesus' place. Here he is, a young man with a rising reputation, and his mother shows up, for crying out loud. Perhaps the crowd snickered: Hey Jesus, your mommy wants you. How embarrassing. Jesus is a young man on the rise, so perhaps he feels a need to distance himself from his family, establish some independence for himself. A harsh tone creeps into his voice. I'll tell you who my mother and brothers are, anyone who does the will of God, that's who. Stick that in yer pipe and puff on it.

Put yourself in Mary's place. Here she took care of Jesus from the moment of his birth, fed and clothed him, stayed up nights with him when he was sick, the whole nine yards until he was finally grown up, and now he ignores her. From her own son, who is the Son of God, she gets the cold shoulder. Kids today have no respect for their elders, even their own aging parents. What's a mother to do?

Does Jesus rush right out to see what his mother wants? Nope. Does he immediately tell the crowd to let his mother and other relatives come in? Nope again. As far as we can tell from the account in Mark's Gospel, Jesus takes advantage of the situation to make a theological point, then it's on to other matters.

Put yourself in Mary's place. Talk about perplexing. This is one perplexing son. She wants a moment of his precious time, and he won't even see her, even talks like being his actual mother counts for less than zero. Anyone who does the will of God can be his mother and brothers and sisters. Great. Just great. This she could do without.

In this familiar but puzzling scene from Mark's Gospel we

encounter the real Mary, the human Mary, not the Mary on many pedestals or the Mary of apparitions. This is not Our Lady of Here, or Our Lady of That. This is Mary the mother of a son who seems to have little concern for her feelings. How many mothers — fathers, too, for that matter — have felt a similar lack of sensitivity from a young adult offspring? This is one of the many things people love about Mary.

But let's not limit the meaning of this story. Listen. Feeling rejected by a loved one — a friend, a relative, whoever — is a universal human experience. To be human, and be involved in human relationships, is to leave oneself open to being hurt, and it happens. It does happen, and Mary has been there. From her own son, yet, she felt rejection and insensitivity. Mary has been there. Has she ever.

What's at stake here is our image of Mary. Sometimes a kind of "magic Mary" takes over. We forget the human Mary who walked the dusty roads of Palestine, who made countless trips back and forth from her home to the village well for water, who prepared endless meals, washed her family's clothes, did all the things a woman did in the culture of her time. Sometimes we forget that at some point Joseph died and Mary became a single mother who had to raise her son by herself. No more "magic Mary."

Holy Mary, pray for me that I may learn to love even when I feel rejected by others. Amen.

Unsettling Mary

Now the birth of Jesus the Messiah took place in this way. When his mother Mary had been engaged to Joseph, but before they lived together, she was found to be with child from the Holy Spirit. (Matthew 1:18)

Thing about the Gospels is this. We put them in the blender of our mind and do a scramble job on them. This means we can overlook the unique perspectives each Gospel offers. We can overlook perspectives, for example, that we might find unsettling. Rather not be unsettled. Goodness, no. Have everything all neat and tidy in my mind, don't want to be unsettled or confused. Goodness, no.

The Gospel of Matthew says zero, zip, nada, about Mary getting a visit from an angel vis-à-vis her impending pregnancy and its special nature. The Gospel of Luke tells us about that, so why be bothered because Matthew says zero, zip, nada? Except maybe Matthew's Gospel *wants* us to be bothered. That's the way the Good News works, you know. It brings a mighty comfort, to be sure. But the gospel also aims to unsettle us. You know. It's the old, old truth of the gospel, to comfort the afflicted and afflict the comfortable. Sometimes we need one, sometimes the other.

So why does Matthew simply say that Mary "was found to be with child from the Holy Spirit" and leave it at that? Why does Matthew stroll up, drop that bomb in our laps, and stroll away with no further comment or explanation? Does he not know that we have our questions and we want some answers? Matthew talks like this sort of thing happens every day, for heaven's sake.

Imagine Matthew thumbing his nose at you. He couldn't care less about our questions. Here it is, he seems to say. Take it or leave it. This sort of thing does not happen every day, Matthew seems to say. But when it did happen, this once, it did not happen for heaven's sake. No. It happened for our sake.

Truth is, the Gospel of Matthew carries the work of a master of understatement. Pedestrian remarks for a pedestrian people. Here is how Jesus was born. Point one: Jesus' mother Mary was engaged to Joseph. Point two: They were not living together yet. Point three, and here things get interesting: Mary became pregnant. Point four, and here things become outrageous: The Holy Spirit was da papa, not Joseph.

Matthew's Gospel has no problem with this. It's as if Matthew says: Well, hey, everyone already knows this. No big deal. How would you expect the Son of God to be conceived? Jesus is fully human, so he has a fully human mother. But he is also fully divine, so he was conceived by the Holy Spirit. You got a problem with that, you got a problem.

Matthew's primary purpose is to tell us who Jesus is, only secondarily who Mary is. His priorities are straight. The early church put two and two together, said hey, we ain't stupid, and gave Mary the title *Theotokos,* Greek for "Mother of God." This title says as much about Jesus as it does about his mother, of course. But the point, ah say the point, when it comes to Mary, is clear. When Mary became pregnant with the Son of God everything was both special and ordinary. Special because the conception took place in a special manner. Ordinary because her pregnancy was a normal human pregnancy.

We are left with a deep reverence for the mystery of

who Jesus is. But we are not left holding the bag. We are also left with a profound sense of awe at who Mary is. *Theotokos.* Mother of God. Mary is one hundred percent human woman, she has no divine-human nature like her son. But she carried the Son of God in her womb for nine months, gave birth to him, nourished him from the fullness of her breasts, raised him, taught him his manners, taught him his prayers, and sent him out into the world. It's enough to bring tears to your eyes.

Holy Mary, Mother of God, pray for me that I may have a greater sensitivity to the presence of the sacred in the ordinary. Amen.

Mary the Favored One

In the sixth month the angel Gabriel was sent by God to a town in Galilee called Nazareth, to a virgin engaged to a man whose name was Joseph, of the house of David. The virgin's name was Mary. And he came to her and said, "Greetings, favored one! The Lord is with you." But she was much perplexed by his words and pondered what sort of greeting this might be.

(Luke 1:26–29)

We have an angel, an angel with a name. Gabriel. The name means "God is strong," a good name for an angel with important things to do for God. In the Book of Daniel, Gabriel interprets dreams, he explains to Daniel the vision of the ram and the male goat (8:16:26). Earlier in Luke's Gospel, Gabriel announces to Zechariah the conception and birth of John who will become the Baptist. Like many angels in the Bible, Gabriel's purpose is to deliver a message from God. Places to go, people to see, things to do. That's an angel for you, and Gabriel can handle the job. Oh yes, he can handle the job.

Luke tells us first that Gabriel was not roaming around on his own. Rather, he was "sent by God." Let's get that much clear from the start. Gabriel is on a special mission from the Creator of the universe here. He is sent by God where? This is important, too. Gabriel is sent by God to "a town in Galilee." A specific place, not someplace-or-other, and the name of the town in Galilee is Nazareth. Luke is very specific about that, and he is specific about that for a reason.

Oh yes, Luke has his reasons. He wants us to know that this important event happened *in the world,* in an ordinary place. Mary did not receive this visit from an angel in some ethereal temple outside of time, away from the knockabout world. No. The message comes from an angel, but it happens in a real place, in an ordinary town. It happens *in the world,* in the same world we inhabit, in a place as ordinary as the places we live. This visit from an angel could have happened anyplace, that's how ordinary Nazareth was. It could have happened in Pittsburgh or Tampa, Seattle, Hong Kong, or Houston. It could have happened in Tucson or Portland, Montreal or Maine, British Columbia or South Carolina. Where it *did* happen was Galilee, in a town called Nazareth, an ordinary place.

We also have a very young woman by modern standards—fourteen, fifteen years old. She has a name, too. Her name is Miriam, but we call her Mary. Luke insists that she is "a virgin," and this observation is as much theological as physiological. Not only is Mary a young, unmarried woman who has never had sexual intercourse, but she wants above all to be open to the word of God. Her virginity is a sign that she is fertile ground for God's word. Mary's virginity is not meant to denigrate sex in marriage. In addition to being how babies are made, no small matter, God designed sexual pleasure as a source of grace for married couples and parents. Sexual pleasure as a source of God's own life, imagine that.

Another thing. The angel Gabriel greets Mary as "favored one," then says, "The Lord is with you." Luke tells us that Mary was "much perplexed" by this and "pondered what sort of greeting this might be." What a fascinating exchange. Mary is not surprised to encounter an angel. Luke does not say, "and she was amazed to see the angel." No. Maybe angel sightings were not unusual in those days. Instead, Mary is "much perplexed" by the angel's words.

Mary's main concern is the message the angel carries from God. At the same time she is not a "blind faith" kind of person. Mary has her questions. Oh yes, she has her questions. Mary stands as a model of faith, a faith that makes room for being perplexed, a faith that leaves time to think about things we don't understand. A faith that never has any questions, doubts, perplexity, is a faith that has lost its fizz.

Holy Mary, pray for me that in living my faith I may leave room to be perplexed and leave time to ponder the meaning of God's word. Amen.

Mary, Young Woman of Faith

The angel said to her, "Do not be afraid, Mary, for you have found favor with God. And now, you will conceive in your womb and bear a son, and you will name him Jesus. He will be great, and will be called the Son of the Most High, and the Lord God will give to him the throne of his ancestor David. He will reign over the house of Jacob forever, and of his kingdom there will be no end. Mary said to the angel, "How can this be, since I am a virgin?" The angel said to her, "The Holy Spirit will come upon you, and the power of the Most High will overshadow you; therefore the child to be born will be holy; he will be called Son of God. And now, your relative Elizabeth in her old age has also conceived a son; and this is the sixth month for her who was said to be barren. For nothing will be impossible with God." Then Mary said, "Here am I, the servant of the Lord; let it be with me according to your word." Then the angel departed from her. (Luke 1:30–38)

This is one of the most dramatic scenes in the entire New Testament. It's enough to take your breath away. First, the angel's words clearly imply that Mary's first response included fear. Mary is afraid. She knows it, and the angel knows it. This is a startling experience, so Gabriel reassures her: "Do not be afraid. . . . " Then the angel announces that young Mary will become the mother of "the Son of the Most High."

You would think that at this point Mary would simply accept the angel's words and acquiesce. But no. Mary has her questions. She knows where babies come from, and she wants to know exactly what's going on and how this conception will take place. Young Mary is not intimidated, even by an angel. She interrogates her heavenly visitor point-blank: "How can this be, since I am a virgin?"

It would be understandable if Gabriel grew impatient. Why can't this young woman just listen to him, accept his message, and do as she is told? Is he an angel or not? But no. She asks a question, and Gabriel shows no impatience at all. He does not say, "Shut up and do as you're told." Gabriel respects Mary and her right to ask questions. Gabriel responds to Mary's question in detail.

Her question answered, Mary replies in the affirmative and in so doing she becomes a model of faith. But take notice. Take notice. Mary is a model of faith not only in her complete acceptance of God's will for her. She is also a model of faith in her questions and curiosity. Her faith does not preclude feeling perplexed, being fearful, and wanting some answers. Mary is not a model of "blind faith." God forbid.

Listen. Young Mary's faith is astonishing. It is a faith which, in the end, says to God, "Whatever you say is fine with me." But it is the faith of a free person, as well, a faith that says, "I know what's what, I know how things work, and I want some information." Ordinarily we do not have such clear, face-to-face dialogues with an angel, of course. God's messages to us more often come through the circumstances and events of everyday life. All the same, we have our questions. We wonder what's going on. We would like some answers, and like young Mary we should not hesitate to ask our questions before we make her words our own: "Here am

I, the servant of the Lord; let it be with me according to your word."

Notice one other fact. The reply young Mary receives to her question is not exactly a crystal-clear, scientifically verifiable explanation. "The Holy Spirit will overshadow you," and so forth, is a reply that heightens the mystery, a reply that itself requires faith to accept. Like Mary, we should not expect crystal-clear responses to our questions. The responses we receive are more likely to heighten the mystery than clear everything up. If you can imagine.

Here is what young Mary teaches us. She teaches us that the mystery itself is trustworthy, for at the heart of the mystery is God's infinite, unconditional love.

Holy Mary, pray for me that I may trust God's love in the mystery of my life. Amen.

Mary, Model for Believers

In those days Mary set out and went with haste to a Judean town in the hill country, where she entered the house of Zechariah and greeted Elizabeth. When Elizabeth heard Mary's greeting, the child leaped in her womb. And Elizabeth was filled with the Holy Spirit and exclaimed with a loud cry, "Blessed are you among women, and blessed is the fruit of your womb. And why has this happened to me, that the mother of my Lord comes to me? For as soon as I heard the sound of your greeting, the child in my womb leaped for joy.

And blessed is she who believed that there would be a fulfillment of what was spoken to her by the Lord."

(Luke 1:39–45)

Mary, Mary, she does not sit still for long. The Gospel of Luke presents her as a young woman of remarkable depth and resilience. She no sooner learns that she will give birth to the Son of the Most High than she travels, lickity-split, to see her elderly cousin. Elizabeth, Elizabeth, how does she know already that Mary is to be "the mother of my Lord"? It's a wonderment, to be sure.

Young Mary is barely in the door, hardly says Shalom, than the infant John in Elizabeth's womb does a flip of joy. Even he, there in his warm, dark chamber, knows that Mary is someone special. This is no mere visit from a neighbor to borrow a cup of flour. For young Mary is "the mother of my Lord." Elizabeth knows it, and the unborn child in her womb knows it. Anybody who is anybody knows it.

Luke's Gospel tells us a most remarkable thing. Elizabeth is "filled with the Holy Spirit." If you can imagine. This phrase, "filled with the Holy Spirit," is unique to the author of the Gospel of Luke and the Acts of the Apostles.

When Luke/Acts describes someone as "filled with the Holy Spirit," that person is inspired by God to speak or act on God's behalf. Even before his birth, John the Baptist is "filled with the Holy Spirit" (Luke 1:15). Zechariah is "filled with the Holy Spirit" when he utters the Benedictus (Luke 1:68–79): "Blessed be the Lord God of Israel, for he has looked favorably on his people and redeemed them. . . . " The apostles are "filled with the Holy Spirit" when they preach in many languages on Pentecost (Acts 2:4).

Elizabeth is "filled with the Holy Spirit," and exclaims "with a loud cry" (very dramatic, is it not?) that Mary is Something Else. Young Mary is "blessed among women," and "blessed" is "the fruit of your womb."

"Blessed" is a word we are so familiar with that we don't pay much attention to it. But look. Look here. To be "blessed" is not just a polite compliment, or a pious formality. Rather — hold onto your hat — to be blessed is to receive a gift of God's own life, and with this gift of divine life come vitality, and strength, and peace. God alone can bless. We can bless only in the sense that we wish and pray that God will bless.

So when Elizabeth, "filled with the Holy Spirit," exclaims "with a loud cry" that Mary is "blessed among women," this is powerful stuff. When Elizabeth declares that the fruit of young Mary's womb is "blessed," that's powerful stuff too. Only Mary is "blessed among women," and only Jesus, the "fruit" of her womb, is "blessed." We are not surprised to learn that Jesus is "blessed." We're talking Son of God here, after all. But it takes a powerful lot to say that Mary, too, is "blessed." This is how the Gospel of Luke tells us that Mary is Something Else and how special is her role in salvation history.

Mary is not a divine being, but she is the mother of the Son of God. Mary is not our Redeemer, but she is the mother of our Redeemer. Mary does not protect us from an angry God. She reminds us about God's maternal love for us. Mary has no power of her own, apart from the power of God. She prays for us as do all the saints. Hence, all those places called "Saint Mary's."

Holy Mary, pray for me that I may grow in my love for you and learn to trust completely in the love of your son, Jesus. Amen.

Magnificat Mary

And Mary said, "My soul magnifies the Lord, and my spirit rejoices in God my Savior, for he has looked with favor on the lowliness of his servant. Surely, from now on all generations will call me blessed; for the Mighty One has done great things for me, and holy is his name. His mercy is for those who fear him from generation to generation. He has shown strength with his arm; he has scattered the proud in the thoughts of their hearts. He has brought down the powerful from their thrones, and lifted up the lowly; he has filled the hungry with good things, and sent the rich away empty. He has helped his servant Israel, in remembrance of his mercy, according to the promise he made to our ancestors, to Abraham and to his descendants forever." (Luke 1:46–55)

Sing it, Mary. Tell us what it's all about. Mary moves center stage, all eyes on her, but she does so not for her own sake, to attract attention to herself, but to remind us who God is and what God's love has done. Here is what I do, Mary says; here is what I do. Like a magnifying glass, God uses me to show the greatness of his love. See, look here. So great is God's love that he will join us in our humanity. So great is God's love that he will be born in the usual manner, come into the world as a helpless infant. I, Mary, what your era calls a "teenager," carry in my womb the Son of the Most High. If you can believe it.

My humility has no limits, Mary sings. Therefore, I rejoice in God who is my Savior. I am lowly, but God has a thing for lowliness. God goes for whatever is lowly. I am God's servant, and he looks with favor on my lowliness, and this is my highest honor. Because God smiles on my lowly status, my emptiness, he fills my soul with light. Therefore, from this day forward everyone will say that I am blessed, filled with divine life. I am lowly, I am human, and all generations will call me blessed.

Sing it, Mary. She is not the center of her own attention. She does not say, "Look at me, look at me." Mary says, "Look at Jesus, look at my son." For the Mighty One has done great things for her, the One whose name is holy. Together, Mary sings, let us love God together.

Sing it, young Mary. You want God's mercy, she sings. You want God's mercy, we all want God's mercy. God is merciful to those who fear him. Fear God? Fear God? We don't know what to do with this. Are we not supposed to love God? What is this "fear God" business? Young Mary does not tell us to be terrified of God. Of course not. To fear God we simply follow her example. We should have a profound respect for God, even allow ourselves to be awestruck now and then. We should worship God with deep respect and devotion. To "fear" God is to obey, love, and trust God.

Why? We should "fear" God, young Mary sings, because God "has shown strength with his arm." Imagine God's arm. What? Is it like the arm pictured on a box of baking soda? Oh Mary, who says you have no sense of humor? Not only that, Mary continues, but here are some magnificent contrasts: Down come powerful folks from their seats of power, up rise those like me, the lowly. The lowly, the lowly, let's hear it for the lowly. A feast for those who are hungry, not so much as a nibble for those who are rich. A feast, a feast, a feast for those who are hungry. That's our God. Sing it, young Mary, sing it.

This is the way things have always been with our God. Remembering mercy, always remembering mercy, this is the way with our God. Always showing mercy to his servant Israel, to his servant Mary, to his servants you, and me, and everyone who calls upon his mercy. If you can imagine that. Sing it, young Mary.

Holy Mary, pray for me that I may worship God with deep respect and rely more completely on God's love and mercy, no matter how difficult life may seem. Amen.

Simple Mary

In those days a decree went out from Emperor Augustus that all the world should be registered. This was the first registration and was taken while Quirinius was governor of Syria. All went to their own towns to be registered. Joseph also went from the town of Nazareth in Galilee to Judea, to the city of David called Bethlehem, because he was descended from the house and family of David. He went to be registered with Mary, to whom he was engaged and who was expecting a child. While they were there, the time came for her to deliver her child. And she gave birth to her firstborn son and wrapped him in bands of cloth, and laid him in a manger, because there was no place for them in the inn.

(Luke 2:1–7)

What else do emperors do? Decree this, decree that, everybody do as you're told. Must have been a real power trip. Luke is at pains to make sure we know that what he is about to tell us really and truly happened. That's why he insists that it happened "when Quirinius was governor of Syria." It doesn't mean a great deal to us, but hey, it meant a lot to Luke's first readers. "Sure, I remember when Quirinius was governor of Syria. What a pain in the patootie that guy was." Luke wanted to make sure everyone knew that the events he was about to narrate were completely historical. "These things happened, folks, I'm not making this up."

So, you remember Joseph? Right, the guy Mary was engaged to. Right, right, that Joseph. He was a law abiding guy, was Joseph. He wanted to do what he was supposed to do. Joseph was engaged to Mary, which in those days was practically as good as being married, so he took her with him, and oh yes, she was expecting a baby. Big time. We're talking way along in the pregnancy here, you bet. But Joseph, he's not worried. Babies are born all the time, right? Right. No big deal. Mary, she's not worried either. Well, maybe a little. She has never given birth before, so, you know, she's not sure what to expect. But she's okay, she knows she can rely on Joseph. What a guy.

So off they trek to Bethlehem, which is where Joseph

must go to register, because Bethlehem is the home town for people descended from the family of David. Which Joseph is. It's all very complicated. Anyway, Mary goes into labor while they are in Bethlehem, and the town is filled to overflowing, not a room to be had. So Mary and Joseph stay in this place where the owner of an inn keeps animals. Hey, it's better than camping alongside the road. That would *really* be the pits.

Mary is fifteen, sixteen years old. Young Mary. Pious legend has Mary riding on a donkey as she and Joseph travel from Nazareth to Bethlehem, but neither Luke nor Matthew mention any such mode of transport. For all we know, Mary walked the same as Joseph. We would like to think she rode on a donkey, great with child as she was, but we'll never know. Could be Mary walked. These were the days when women gave birth and went back to work an hour later. Maybe it would have been considered namby-pamby to ride a donkey. Maybe Mary and Joseph were too poor to afford a donkey. Who knows?

Luke is short and to the point. While Mary and Joseph were in Bethlehem, Mary gave birth to "her child." There is a wonder here. Luke does not say that Mary gave birth to the Savior of the World — although this is clearly true. He simply says that Mary gave birth to "her child." It's nice, homey, beautiful the way it is. The holy in the ordinary.

Mary, who would go on to bigger and better things because of giving birth to "her child," for the moment is simply a young woman with her baby, trying to get comfortable in a place where animals — cows, maybe; pigs, maybe; donkeys, maybe — are the only source of heat. Imagine that. There lies the infant Christ in a manger, a feedbox for animals, and there is his mother. She looks from her baby to Joseph and back again. She is happy. She is tired, and she smiles. She is glad that Joseph is there.

Holy Mary, pray for me that I may take comfort in the simple things. Amen.

Contemplative Mary

So [the shepherds] went with haste and found Mary and Joseph, and the child lying in the manger. When they saw this, they made known what had been told them about this child; and all who heard it were amazed at what the shepherds told them. But Mary treasured all these words and pondered them in her heart.

(Luke 2:16–19)

How can such a short little snippet from a Gospel have so much packed into it? Amazements from horizon to horizon, amazements right between the eyes. So look. Look.

These are the characters: Shepherds, an indeterminate number, could be two, could be twenty. Mary, the mama. Joseph, for all practical purposes the papa. The child, cause of all the fuss. Other people — strangers, passers-by of indeterminate number, age, and sex.

The scene: a stable, or a cave, or a lean-to, impossible to say, but a place of some kind next to an inn, where the innkeeper keeps certain animals about which no details are available.

Here come the shepherds, two or twenty, they screech to a halt in the entryway, or door, or whatever. They have been running as fast as their legs could carry them. They pant, breathing hard. Astonishing experience out there in the sheep-populated fields just a while ago, what with an angel, the heavenly host, glory and all. Enough to make anyone do a four-minute mile. So listen, they say to Mary and Joseph, their eyes glued to the baby in the manger. So listen. An angel, and glory, and the heavenly host, out there in the fields (pant, pant) . . . angel with a message, and here's the (pant, pant) message: This baby is the Savior, the Messiah and Lord. That's what the angel said, it's what the angel said.

Mary says nothing. Joseph says nothing. The animals in the stable, or cave, or lean-to, are mum. The child in the manger makes not a sound. The shepherds, two or twenty, stumble back into the alley, or street, or path, or whatever. They describe their experience and tell the message to whoever they see, and whoever they see is amazed, absolutely. Amazements all over the place for an indeterminate number of strangers and passers-by. Absolutely.

People falling all over themselves, shepherds and strangers. Amazements by the dozen. Meanwhile, back in the stable, or cave, or lean-to, Mary heard what the shepherds, two or twenty, said. Luke does not say that Mary is amazed. Maybe since a certain Gabriel angel visited her about nine months earlier she is hard to amaze, having already had the ultimate amazement. Mary is not amazed. Joseph is silent, thinking about who knows what, certain dreams maybe.

Mary heard what the shepherds said, and what does she do? Mary is not amazed, she is quiet. She "treasured all these words and pondered them in her heart." Treasuring and pondering — not in your head but in your heart. Luke suggests that this is a grand idea. Amazed is fine, but treasuring and pondering in your heart is better. Treasuring and pondering in your heart, like young Mary.

There is another word for treasuring and pondering, a four-syllable word. The word is "contemplative." Don't let it startle you. Everyone does it. Common as dirt, more valuable than diamonds. To be a contemplative is to treasure and ponder. Or cherish and meditate upon. Everyone does this, just about. But *what* do we cherish and meditate upon? Do we cherish and meditate upon stuff we don't have, a nicer car, newer furniture, the endless stream of stuff on a television shopping network? Do we, perchance, cherish and meditate upon our worries and anxieties?

Or do we cherish and meditate upon what young Mary treasured and pondered in her heart after the frantic visit of the shepherds, two or twenty? Hm?

Holy Mary, pray for me that I may learn how to be quiet. Amen.

Amazed Mary

Now there was a man in Jerusalem whose name was Simeon; this man was righteous and devout, looking forward to the consolation of Israel, and the Holy Spirit rested on him. It had been revealed to him by the Holy Spirit that he would not see death before he had seen the Lord's Messiah. Guided by the Spirit, Simeon came into the temple; and when the parents brought in the child Jesus, to do for him what was customary under the law, Simeon took him in his arms and praised God, saying, "Master, now you are dismissing your servant in peace, according to your word; for my eyes have seen your salvation, which you have prepared in the presence of all peoples, a light for revelation to the Gentiles and for glory to your people Israel." And the child's father and mother were amazed at what was being said about him. Then Simeon blessed them and said to his mother Mary, "This child is destined for the falling and the rising of many in Israel, and to be a sign that will be opposed so that the inner thoughts of many will be revealed — and a sword will pierce your own soul too."

(Luke 2:25–35)

A most remarkable moment in the temple. Old Simeon, he is old, but his mind is clear, his mind rings like a bell when the young couple approaches, the young woman carrying a baby. Don't let the ancient visage fool you. Don't let the shuffling step and stooped figure fool you. Simeon's mind is as clear as a bell; he knows that he will not pass over the great divide until he sees the Messiah.

Day after day, for as long as anyone can remember, Simeon drifts about the temple, his old arms raised in prayer, but day after day there is no Messiah. All he sees are ordinary people, the usual temple traffic. But today is different. Simeon lays eyes on Mary, Joseph, and the child Jesus, and bingo. His patience has paid off. This child, this one, this one is the Messiah, he knows it in his heart, it rings in his mind like a bell. He approaches, he takes the child in his arms, then he speaks the most remarkable prayer. For he sees eternal love in the eyes of a smiling, gurgling infant. Simeon speaks of Jesus as "a light to the Gentiles... for glory to your people Israel." This baby, which he takes in his arms so carefully, with such love, is light for the Gentiles, the non-chosen people. Of all things. But this same baby brings golden glory to the people from which he comes, the people called Israel. Clear as a bell.

Simeon prays, his old eyes bright with joy, and the young couple, Joseph and Mary, don't know what to do. Their mouths hang open in astonishment. What on earth? After all that has happened, the announcement from the Gabriel angel, the message from the shepherds, you would think that Mary and Joseph would be hard to astonish. But they are flabbergasted at Simeon's words. Well, it is understandable. Yes, the Gabriel angel said what he said, and yes, the shepherds said what they said. But a baby is a baby, and new parents are new parents, and it's all so difficult to grasp. Simeon's words amaze them, and it is understandable. Mary and Joseph have a lot to learn.

To cap things off, Simeon lays a blessing on Joseph and Mary, which is nice. But then he lays an even more astonishing — frightening even — message on the young couple. Simeon says that this little baby has a destiny, something about the rising and falling of many in Israel. What on earth? Something about the baby being a sign that will be opposed, and the inner thoughts of many people being revealed. What? Then Simeon looks directly at Mary and says that a sword will pierce her soul. My Lord. It's frightening. The future can be so frightening. Mary has had more preparation for ongoing remarkables than most. Still, with Joseph she continues to be amazed and perplexed. And so do we.

Holy Mary, pray for me that I may love God with all my heart. Amen.

Family Mary

Now every year [Jesus'] parents went to Jerusalem for the festival of the Passover. And when he was twelve years old, they went up as usual for the festival. When the festival was ended and they started to return, the boy Jesus stayed behind in Jerusalem, but his parents did not know it. Assuming that he was in the group of travelers, they went a day's journey. Then they started to look for him among their relatives and friends. When they did not find him, they returned to Jerusalem to search for him. After three days they found him in the temple, sitting among the teachers, listening to them and asking them questions. And all who heard him were amazed at his understanding and his answers. When his parents saw him they were astonished; and his mother said to him, "Child, why have you treated us like this? Look, your father and I have been search-ing for you in great anxiety." He said to them, "Why were you searching for me? Did you not know that I must be in my Father's house?" But they did not understand what he said to them. Then he went down with them and came to Nazareth, and was obedient to them. His mother treasured all these things in her heart.

(Luke 2:41–51)

A most remarkable story. The only account we have, in any of the Gospels, of an interaction between the members of the Holy Family, and what is it but a story of anxiety, conflict and reconciliation. So appropriate, for this is what so much of family life consists of — anxiety, conflict and reconciliation. Mary, she knows. She has been there, as this story illustrates. It's enough to bring tears to your eyes.

Think about it. Let us knock off some of the golden patina of piety that frequently obstructs our view of this familiar story. The Holy Family is off to the festival of the Passover. They do this every year, they have been doing it since Jesus was a baby. Maybe it was like the annual family vacation. Now the festival is over, and Jesus decides that he is not ready to go home. Not just yet. What was he thinking? Did he plan to make the trek home all by himself next week? What did he plan to do about meals? Where did he plan to sleep? Like a typical twelve-year-old, the boy Jesus didn't think ahead about the consequences of his actions. He also, apparently, did not have much concern about his parents' feelings. Did he think about the fact that they would worry?

Mary and Joseph, for their part, headed for home unconcerned. Maybe this kind of thing had happened before. Plenty of friends and relatives, Jesus often hung out with them; it's one of the advantages of the extended family. At the end of the first day of travel, however, Mary and Joseph go looking for Jesus and find that he is gone. What do you mean you thought he was with me? I thought he was with you! So, back they go to Jerusalem. Holy mackerel, we left our only child behind at the campground.

So, that's one day's journey away, another day's journey back, and Luke says it was only after three days that Mary and Joseph found Jesus, so they spend a third day searching. Well, think about it. Mary and Joseph must have been just about frantic by now. Where did we see him last? Where did *anyone* see him last? Have you seen our son? He's twelve years old, about this tall, and he was wearing this and that, and...No? Thanks, anyway. Have you seen our son? He's twelve years old, about this tall, and he was wearing this and that, and...No? Okay, thanks anyway. Have you seen our son? Have you seen our son? Have you seen...?

Finally, at the end of the third day they find him in, of all places, the temple, being a whiz kid. Luke tells us that Mary and Joseph are "astonished." Why? Notice, they looked for three days before they thought to look in the temple. The temple was not the first place they thought Jesus might be. They are astonished to find him there. What does this tell us about Jesus? Maybe that Jesus was no holier-than-thou kind of kid. Whoa. Imagine that.

Mary puts it to him point blank: "Child," she calls him. "Child, why have you treated us like this? Look, your father and I have been searching for you in great anxiety." Worried half to death. You can imagine. And what does Mary get? A contrite son? An apology? Chagrin? Hardly.

Mary and Joseph get a smart-mouth adolescent comeback, that's what they get. It's all in the tone of voice, which Luke tells us nothing about, but pay close attention and read between the lines. Jesus' response to Mary's expression of anxiety is to ignore it. Jesus asks why Mary and Joseph had bothered to look for him at all. He says that he had things to do of his own. Then Luke says that Mary and Joseph hadn't a clue about the meaning of Jesus' response. Not a clue. Very like the parents of many an adolescent child who don't have a clue about what their kids are up to. What they do know is "great anxiety."

All the same, Jesus gets up and follows his parents home again. Not, we may surmise, without some choice comments along the way about not treating him like a baby anymore. Luke tells us Jesus was "obedient to them," but not a word about his attitude. We can only guess. But Mary, she does not forget a thing. "His mother treasured all these things in her heart." How like a mother, nothing unusual, really. Is this not what mothers — fathers, too, for that matter — do? Treasure all these things in their hearts? Of course it is. Mary has been there. She knows.

Holy Mary, pray for me that I may learn to treasure the events of my life in my heart and find there the mystery of God's love for me. Amen.

Mary the Wedding Guest

On the third day there was a wedding in Cana of Galilee, and the mother of Jesus was there. Jesus and his disciples had also been invited to the wedding. When the wine gave out, the mother of Jesus said to him, "They have no wine." (John 2:1–3)

If Jewish weddings were anything in Jesus' day like Jewish weddings are today, this was not an event to be missed. John's Gospel tells us first that "the mother of Jesus was there." Only then do we learn that "Jesus and his disciples had also been invited." This isn't exactly an afterthought, but all the same John's Gospel mentions "the mother of Jesus" first.

Think about it. Here is Mary at a wedding. How fun. It's a grand party, the bride is beautiful, the groom is handsome, and the party is in full swing. Music and dancing. Do you think Mary sat in a corner polishing her halo? Do you think she sat there like a bump on a log or a professional wallflower? That would be hard to imagine. If she noticed that the wine was all gone, you can be sure she sipped a few herself in honor of the occasion. Mary at a wedding enjoys the music. Mary at a wedding joins in the dancing. Mary at a wedding rejoices with the bride and groom, and she wishes them well.

Did men and women dance together in the Jewish culture of the time? Maybe no, maybe yes. Let's imagine yes. Just for the fun of it, let's imagine yes. If the religious culture allowed for it, the real Mary, the Mary who told an angel that God could count on her, this Mary would dance the night away. The real Mary lived life, she didn't let it pass her by. Imagine. Maybe Mary at a wedding dances with Jesus, her son! Why not? Mary has a good time. She enjoys herself. She dances, dances, kicks up her heels with Jesus, her son. Why not?

Oh my Lord, Mary and Jesus dancing at a wedding.

Maybe, just to be polite, she dances with some of Jesus' disciples, too. Mary dancing with Peter. Wow. What a hoot. When it came to dancing, Peter probably had two left feet, but Mary dances with him all the same. What fun! The Blessed Virgin Mary and the good-hearted klutz who would be the first Pope, as it were, dancing at a wedding in Cana of Galilee. Mother of Jesus, dance. Dance, St. Peter, dance. You can do it, fella.

There is a lesson here — probably more than one lesson, but we'll settle for one. The mother of the Son of God, Jesus the Son of God, and the disciples of Jesus, they all attend a wedding. They celebrate love, they all believe that the love of husband and wife deserves a party. They all believe that the beginning of a marriage is worth dancing for, worth sipping the fruit of the vine for. There is a lesson here, and the lesson is this: Human love is something God finds irresistible. When one human being loves another human being, "Gotta be there," God whispers to the angels. "Outta my way, gotta be there," exclaims the Creator of the universe.

God goes for human love — in this Cana case the love of a young man and woman — like a bear goes for honey: gimme more, gimme more, gimme more. God loves going to weddings, can't miss a one. Even the ones that "don't work out," God can't resist being there anyway out of sheer, limitless, even foolish hope. God hopes for the best, the Creator of the universe can't resist a wedding.

Because God can't resist human love, even human romantic love, the Mother of God can't resist it, either. Mary, the Queen of the Universe, loves to attend a wedding. She looks out for the concerns of the bride and the groom, speaks up for them to Jesus, her son. They have no wine. They need a place to live. They don't have a job. They want to have a baby. They are having trouble paying their bills. They have no wine, they have no wine. Jesus listens, and the wine is forthcoming.

Holy Mary, Mother of God, help me to recognize opportunities for laughter and joy; pray for me that I may enjoy life as you enjoyed life. Amen.

Mary at the Cross

Meanwhile, standing near the cross of Jesus were his mother, and his mother's sister, Mary the wife of Clopas, and Mary Magdalene. When Jesus saw his mother and the disciple whom he loved standing beside her, he said to his mother, "Woman, here is your son." Then he said to the disciple, "Here is your mother." And from that hour the disciple took her into his own home. (John 19:25b–27)

A poignant scene, probably the most poignant scene in the entire New Testament. Here is what a mother's hopes and dreams have come to, a son horribly executed for being a perceived threat to the Roman authorities. Mary and three other women stand "near the cross." Think of stories you have heard about women whose sons were executed for some terrible crime they committed. The heartache such women know at the time of their son's execution is impossible for anyone else to fathom. Now imagine that the son is innocent of any crime....

The four women stand together near the cross, watching. They do not stand apart from one another, they stand with their arms around one another, they embrace, they comfort one another. They do not speak unless it is to pray prayers of sorrow, crying to God. Crying to God, perhaps, about the injustice of it all. Who is to know?

Mary and the three other women stand near the cross. Four women stand and watch and wait. What else can they do? But they are used to waiting, they have been waiting all their lives. They know what it is to wait, so they wait. What else can they do? Four women. But there is at least one man there, too — "the disciple whom [Jesus] loved." Tradition identifies this man as John himself, with whom the Fourth Gospel originated. A particularly close friend of Jesus, the beloved disciple stands near the cross, as well, with Mary and the three other women. He, too, stands watching and waiting. What else can he do? What else?

Jesus hangs on the cross, his suffering profound. But he is not blinded by his suffering, he is not self-absorbed, even as his body is wracked by pain he is not self-absorbed. Jesus knows that his suffering has value, has meaning. In this, he teaches us that no suffering is without meaning, mysterious though it be. Even in our suffering, Jesus is with us.

Jesus' mother stands near the cross, and Jesus sees her. His eyes meet her's. Jesus sees his old friend, as well. Even on the cross he can see that his mother will be alone now. Even as waves of pain pulse through his body, Jesus thinks of his mother, of her needs after his death.

The most remarkable event, the most remarkable event

perhaps in the history of the world. Jesus, nailed to the wood of the cross, speaks. Jesus speaks from the cross, and his words do not express complaint. He does not beg someone to hasten his end. He speaks to his mother, and his words are clear. He speaks to his close friend, and his words are clear. Be together, he tells his mother and his friend. Be mother and son to each other, he tells his mother and his friend. Be together, do not be alone, be together.

The Mary of this poignant scene in the Fourth Gospel is silent. She stands, she waits, and in the end she accepts the hospitality of her son's friend, who "took her into his home." Could be, could be, that this is the Mary we find most commonly today. In a sense. Perhaps today Mary stands and waits and hopes to be taken into our homes, as well. Think of the beloved disciple as representing all of us. Jesus gives his mother to us as our mother, too. She is our mother, and we are her daughters and sons. Together with Mary, the Blessed Mother, we stand near the cross. Together with Mary, our Blessed Mother, we welcome into our lives the power of her son's Resurrection.

Holy Mary, pray for me that I may be close to Jesus, even in heartache and pain; help me to welcome the power of his Resurrection. Amen.

Mary at Prayer

When they had entered the city, they went to the room upstairs where they were staying, Peter, and John, and

James, and Andrew, Philip and Thomas, Bartholomew
and Matthew, James son of Alphaeus, and Simon the
Zealot, and Judas son of James. All these were constantly devoting themselves to prayer, together with
certain women, including Mary the mother of Jesus...
(Acts 1:13-14)

The final mention of Mary in the New Testament. The last
time any New Testament document refers to her explicitly.
It has been quite a day, what with the Ascension of Jesus,
and the angel telling the disciples to go back and wait for the
Holy Spirit and all. So the disciples of Jesus wait, together
they wait for they know not what. Waiting, waiting.

All those male names: Peter, his name always comes first,
indicating some form of priority, followed by John, James,
Andrew, Philip, Thomas, Bartholomew, Matthew, James, Simon the Zealot, and Judas son of James, sometimes called
Jude. All those men, and what are they doing? Praying.
We tend to interpret this in pious ways. Oh my, there they
are, the disciples of Jesus, caught up in highly contemplative
prayer, mysticism of some kind, holiness all over the place.
But maybe that's not accurate.

These people are terrified. They don't know what's going on, and they don't know what to expect. What is this
Holy Spirit they are supposed to wait for? When will it
come? When we read that the disciples are constantly devoting themselves to prayer, this is probably the prayer of a
frightened and uncertain group begging God to help them.
Lord, Lord.

The Acts of the Apostles tells us that, oh yes, "certain
women" are there also, but the only one named is "Mary the

mother of Jesus." Even this early in the history of the Christian community Mary rates special mention; she has a unique status in the community as the mother of Jesus. Think about it. Mary is the only one who was present from day one. From the conception of Jesus, through his childhood and adolescence, during the time of his public ministry, she was with Jesus. Mary was there at the cross when Jesus died, she has been there ever since, and now she waits. Mary waits with all those men for Pentecost, the birth of the church.

Mary is not only the mother of Jesus, the Son of God, she is also the ultimate model of discipleship, and she knows how to wait. She knows that being a disciple of Jesus often means waiting for Lord knows what. Did the frightened, impatient, uncertain disciples turn to Mary for reassurance as they prayed? Did they look to her for encouragement, the kind of encouragement only a mother can give? Did Mary take on a "mother-figure" role among the disciples as they waited and prayed? Luke, the author of the Acts of the Apostles, does not say.

The New Testament authors never did anything by accident or for no reason in particular. Oh, no. Mary appears here for a reason, because she was a significant presence not only in a significant event in the church's past, but in the church of the late second century when Luke wrote his Gospel and the Acts of the Apostles. Mary figures prominently both in Luke and Acts because she figured prominently in the life and faith of the community of faith for which Luke did his writing.

Mary, Mary, mother of Jesus, mother of the Messiah, *Theotokos* (Mother of God), and our mother, too. It was crucial for the early church to remember Mary. Among other things, to remember Mary is to remember the humanity of Jesus, and this is what she does in Luke/Acts. As the human mother of Jesus, she reminds us that Jesus was fully human as well as fully divine. In her response to God's will for her, she also stands as the ideal model of what it means to be a follower of Christ, to say yes to God's will in all things. Yes to God's will no matter how difficult or impossible it may be to understand. Yes to God's will. Not without some questions, perhaps; not without some puzzlement, perhaps; but, in the end, yes. In all things.

Holy Mary, pray for me that I may rejoice in my humanity and follow God's will in all things. Amen.

MARY IN THE LITURGY

Mary, Mother of God (January 1)

> We turn to you for protection, holy Mother of God. Listen to our prayers and help us in our needs. Save us from every danger, glorious and blessed Virgin.
> — *The Oldest Known Prayer to Mary*

Apart from the "Hail Mary," this is the oldest known prayer to the Blessed Virgin. Called the "Sub Tuum Praesidium," it was discovered some years ago on a papyrus in Egypt and is dated to the early fourth century. This prayer brings us into the presence of an early Christian community and echoes this primitive faith community's devotion to Mary.

Now look. This ancient prayer is not a private prayer, it does not begin with "I," it begins with "we." This is a prayer prayed together by a faith community, probably in a liturgical context. The feast of Mary we observe on January 1 brings her before the whole church, the whole people of God, and we recall that she is what the early church called her, in Greek *Theotokos*, which literally means something like "Birth-Giver of God," or "God bearer," or "Bringer-forth-of-God."

It may come as a surprise, then, to hear that one of the main reasons the church insists that Mary is the Mother, or "Birth-Giver," of God is because it is so important to preserve our awareness of her *humanity* and that of Jesus, son of Mary and Son of God. Mary of Nazareth, ordinary looking wife and mother in first-century Palestine, is the Mother of God. Jesus of Nazareth, ordinary looking young Jewish son, is also the Son of the Most High. It's enough to knock you for a loop, when you think about it. Mary, Mary, making the daily trip to and from the village well, dusty feet and all, is the Mother of God. Jesus, Jesus, learning from Joseph the carpenter's craft, is the Son of God. That's what *Theotokos* is all about, humanity and divinity embracing, coming together to celebrate each other, the best and most intimate of friends.

On the first day of January, on the first day of a new year, we whistle up Mary, the Mother of God, and what do we discover, to our delight? Do we find the Mary of great, classic paintings, Mary floating above clouds, her garments billowing against a royal blue sky? Nah. On the first day of January, on the first day of a new year, we discover a Mary contrary to all that. We find ourselves face-to-face with a Mary who looks as if she is the farthest thing in the world from the Mother of God. She looks so utterly ordinary, yet so strong, so full of love and compassion and delight in us, who are her children. Precisely because she is this ordinary kind of Mary, she is also the glorious Mother of God.

Holy Mary, pray for us that we may be ordinary enough to be holy. Amen.

March 25 – The Annunciation of the Lord
   (See pp. 22–27 above.)
May 31 – The Visitation of the Virgin Mary to Elizabeth
   (See pp. 27–30 above.)

Our Lady of Mount Carmel (July 16)

The patronal feast of the Carmelite Order was originally the Assumption of the Blessed Virgin Mary on August 15; but between 1376 and 1386 the custom arose of observing a special feast of our Lady, to celebrate the approval of their rule by Pope Honorius III in 1226. This custom appears to have originated in England; and the observance was fixed for July 16, which is also the date that, according to Carmelite tradition, our Lady appeared to St. Simon Stock and gave him the scapular. At the beginning of the seventeenth century it became definitely the "scapular feast" and soon began to be observed outside the order. In 1726 this feast day was extended to the whole Western church by Pope Benedict XIII.

— Butler's Lives of the Saints, vol. III

The feast of Our Lady of Mount Carmel is a marvel. Why on earth is it there? The basic story is cut-and-dried. The Blessed Mother appeared to Saint Simon Stock and gave him the brown scapular — the sleeveless outer garment that hangs from the shoulders, front and back, worn in this case by members of the Carmelite order. End of story, and it doesn't have much of a plot. . . . But more about this anon.

Saint Simon Stock is another matter entirely, his life and character the stuff — literally — of legend. Reputedly living to the age of 100 before he died at Bordeaux, France, on May 16, 1265, Simon was called "Stock" because when he was but a boy living in his native Kent, England, he chose the life of a hermit and made his home in the hollow trunk of a tree. Eventually, Simon made his way to the Holy Land, where he joined the primitive Carmelites living on Mount Carmel. When persecution by the Saracens made life there impossible, Simon returned with his community to Kent where he was elected superior-general in 1247.

Returning to the legendary elements of Simon's story, it seems that he was a strict vegetarian. One day his brethren offered him a cooked fish to eat, but Simon ordered that the fish be thrown into the river, whereupon the cooked fish flipped its fins and swam away restored to life. Now that's a story worth repeating.

Saint Simon Stock's time as superior-general of the Carmelites was filled with remarkable developments. He established Carmelite houses in four university towns — Cambridge, Oxford, Paris, and Bologna, which resulted in a large number of young men joining the order. St. Simon also established many foundations in England, Ireland, and perhaps Scotland, Spain, and various other European countries. By now, the Carmelites had switched from being hermits to living as mendicant, or begging, friars, so in 1247 Pope Innocent IV approved a new Carmelite rule. A few years later he also issued a letter of protection for the Carmelites because they were being harassed by various members of the clergy who at this time were jealous of the highly successful Dominicans.

It was during this stressful time that the story went about that the Blessed Mother had appeared to Simon Stock and gave him the brown scapular. As the story went, Mary appeared to Simon holding the scapular of the order in her hand, and she said, "This shall be a privilege unto thee and all Carmelites; he who dies in this habit shall be saved."

Once again, however, we may be in the realm of the legendary for the evidence for the historicity of this event is slim at best. There are no documents from the time of Saint Simon Stock attesting to its factuality. On the other hand, the wearing of the brown scapular, and a miniature version of it in the form of two little patches of cloth on strings, worn over the shoulders under one's clothing, became a widespread devotion encouraged by several popes.

Saint Simon Stock's devotion to Mary is beyond question. Although Simon was never formally canonized, and his name is not in the Roman Martyrology, his feast is celebrated with permission of Vatican authorities in the Carmelite Order and in the English Dioceses of Birmingham, Northampton, and Southwark. After Simon's death in 1265, we are told that many miracles occurred near his grave at Bordeaux. In 1951, what remained of his body — after nearly 700 years darn little, one may presume — was solemnly moved to the restored Carmelite friary at Aylesford, in Kent, England.

The story of Our Lady of Mount Carmel is, then, more the story of Saint Simon Stock since we hear little from or about the Blessed Mother. She puts in a brief appearance of a probably fictional nature, speaks a few words, also of a probably fictional nature, and that's the end of that. So what are we to learn from the Feast of Our Lady of Mount Carmel? Perhaps only this, that devotion to the Blessed Mother, down through the centuries, has had a tremendous impact on many different people and various religious communities. This devotion fires the Catholic imagination in unpredictable but frequently delightful ways.

In the end, we are left with the insight that Mary's prayerful protection is a heart-warming reality that pops up at the most unexpected times and in the most unexpected places.

Our Lady of Mount Carmel, pray for us. Amen.

Dedication of the Basilica of St. Mary Major in Rome (August 5)

In the 13th century the legend of the founding of the basilica of St. Mary Major popularized this local memorial under the title of the "Dedication of the Blessed Virgin Mary of the Snows." The feast was introduced into the Roman calendar in 1568.

—from the *Liturgy of the Hours*

Scattered around the earth like stars across a summer sky you will find churches named in honor of Mary, the mother of Jesus. In the tiniest towns and the largest cities, in urban and suburban areas, you will find churches named in honor of the Blessed Mother. Something there is in the Catholic heart that loves to name a church for the mother of Jesus.

The Feast of the Dedication of the Basilica of St. Mary Major landed on the Roman liturgical calendar because this particular church has some pride of place. It was the first church in Rome dedicated to the mother of Jesus: *Santa Maria Maggiore,* Great St. Mary's.

St. Mary Major, located on Rome's Esquiline Hill, was actually the third of what are known as the patriarchal basilicas to be built in Rome. Originally constructed during the pontificate of Pope Liberius, in the fourth century, the church was first called the "Liberian Basilica." The church was restored and rededicated to the Virgin Mary by Pope Sixtus III, about the year 435.

Remarkably, the liturgical books call the basilica of St. Mary Major "St. Mary of the Snows." This comes from a popular tradition which declares that Mary chose this place for a church dedicated to her by causing a miraculous summer snowfall on the spot where the basilica is now located. According to the tradition, Mary appeared to a wealthy man named John who generously founded and endowed the church during the fourth-century pontificate of Pope Liberius.

Charming legend, probably only that, for we find no mention of this miracle until 100 years after it was supposed to have happened. To add to the legendary aura of the basilica, it is also sometimes called St. Mary *ad Praesepe* because it houses an alleged relic of the crib or manger in which the infant Jesus was laid at his birth. Also highly unlikely... but charming all the same, and why not?

The fact that a church would be named for Mary as early as 435 attests to the power of devotion to Mary in the early Christian communities. To name a beautiful basilica for Mary is but an echo of the admiration and love Christians had for her from the earliest days. In "Annunciation," a poem in her book *A Door in the Hive*, Denise Levertov gives modern expression to the kinds of perceptions that must have inspired a basilica such as St. Mary Major. First Denise Levertov describes the scene of the Annunciation, then continues:

She had been a child who played, ate, slept
like any other child — but unlike others,
wept only for pity, laughed
in joy not triumph.
Compassion and intelligence
fused in her, indivisible.

Called to a destiny more momentous
than any in all of Time,
she did not quail,
        only asked
a simple, "How can this be?"
and gravely, courteously,
took to heart the angel's reply,
perceiving instantly
the astounding ministry she was offered:

to bear in her womb
Infinite weight and lightness; to carry
in hidden, finite inwardness,
nine months of Eternity; to contain
in slender vase of being,
the sum power —
in narrow flesh,
the sum of light.
        Then bring to birth,
push out into air, a Man-child
needing, like any other,
milk and love —
but who was God...

Early, early, in Christian history people grasped intuitively the faith and courage of Mary. They saw her as a model for their own faith and so were inclined to name their churches in her honor. It's a wonderful truth, a beautiful and inspiring historical fact.

Holy Mary, pray for me that I may be guided by your example and helped by your prayers. Amen.

Assumption of the Virgin Mary Into Heaven (August 15)

We pronounce, declare, and define it to be a divinely revealed dogma: that the Immaculate Mother of God, the ever Virgin Mary, having completed the course of her earthly life, was assumed body and soul into heavenly glory.

— Pope Pius XII,
Munificentissimus Deus (November 1, 1950)

There is a wonderful poem, in Brooke Horvath's book *Consolation at Ground Zero,* called "Madonna of the Paintings." In this poem history is short-circuited and overlaps with itself. Mary "thinks she's looking good again, / the way she looked when she was single, / her face in the window's mirror / a portrait by Botticelli or Richard Avedon, / though this has, she suspects, / something to do with the odd light / now constantly gathering about her, / its intense, painterly quality."

Later in the poem, Mary complains that "the paintings all look / much the same to her, their titles silly / and unimaginative — *Madonna of the Goldfinch*, / *Madonna of the Fish*, *Madonna with Angels*. / There must be three dozen called *Madonna and Child* / (she put a stop to that — all that sitting around / was not good for a small boy). / Now she sends Jesus down to the store, / or out to help his father plane and varnish, / whenever some Italian or German-speaking genius / arrives with his brushes and apprentices / to pose her 'just so' in her favorite chair...."

Brooke Horvath's poem plays with time and circumstance the way a child plays with building blocks, mixing them up to make all kinds of pretty patterns as they tower into the air and tumble to the floor. This is what belief in the Assumption of Mary is about, as well. It simply says that what will happen to us all happened to Mary with no regard for historical progression, no regard for the usual intersection of time and space. The doctrine of the Assumption does not say whether Mary experienced death or not, prior to her Assumption. We are free to believe either that she died or did not die, before God took her whole person, "body and soul," into eternity.

Oh, Mary, Mary, Mary. Why do we rob you of your humanity by the ways we interpret doctrines? Official church doctrines are meant to reveal truth, not sweep it under a rug. We say that you were "assumed" into heaven body and soul, an act of God, whereas Jesus "ascended" into heaven, which was an act of his own. The Feast of the Assumption, then, is a time to give glory to God for the special blessings you received. It's a time to focus on the One who did for you in a remarkable manner what will be done for all of us, as well.

For we, too, in God's good time will be "assumed" body and soul into heaven. That's what the doctrine of the resurrection of the body is about.

And yet...And yet...Let's not wander into a theological Ding-Dong School, here. The Assumption of Mary is a mystery beyond time and space. Sometimes our modern scientific mindset hinders as much as it helps. Whoa, we say. Wish I could have been there with a video camera to record the event. Such a video would sell today like hot cakes at a Boy Scout breakfast. I'd be a millionaire. I'd be a billionaire!

Sorry, but it just ain't so. Quoth Carmelite Father Kilian Healy in *The Assumption of Mary* (1982), "...the Assumption is outside the domain of the historian and of natural scientists. Television cameras at the time of Mary's passage from this world would have been useless."

Does this mean that Mary's Assumption never really happened? Of course not. Tradition favors that she did experience death. Most of the Fathers of the Church believed that Mary died, and the great scholastic theologians of the Middle Ages taught the same. So, if Mary died and a television camera would have been useless in recording her Assumption, what exactly was the Assumption? It was a real event in which history was short-circuited and overlapped with itself....

Holy Mary, pray for me that I may share in the life of eternity now and at the hour of my death. Amen.

Queenship of the Virgin Mary
(August 22)

> Hail, Queen of the heavens!
> Hail, Empress of the angels!
> Hail, Root of Jesse, gate of morn!
> From you the world's true Light was born...
>
> — From the *Ave Regina Coelorum*
> (12th century)

Images of Mary, Queen of heaven, the work of the artist's craft — statues, paintings, drawings, stained glass windows — typically portray Mary with a crown on her head. Fair enough. The crown is a sign of royalty, and your average queen will don a crown on ceremonial occasions. Fair enough. But let's be playful. Let's imagine a delightful, playful Queen of Heaven who does not forget the joy of being human, who never ever forgets. Let's just imagine....

In her novel *Divine Secrets of the Ya-Ya Sisterhood*, Rebecca Wells suggests a frisky, playful Mary, Queen of Heaven. Her central character, Siddalee Walker, is a girl age six, living "in the hot heart of Louisiana." Sidda awakens in the night from "a mean dream," then she leaves her house and "walks barefoot into the humid night, moonlight on her freckled shoulders." Rebecca Wells continues:

> Near a huge, live oak tree on the edge of her father's cotton fields, Sidda looks up into the sky. In the crook of the crescent moon sits the Holy Lady, with strong muscles and a merciful heart. She kicks her splendid legs like the moon is her swing and the sky, her front porch.

She waves down at Sidda like she has just spotted an old buddy.

Sidda stands in the moonlight and lets the Blessed Mother love every hair on her six-year-old head. Tenderness flows down from the moon and up from the earth. For one fleeting, luminous moment, Sidda Walker knows there has never been a time when she has not been loved.

Let us have this sort of Mary, Queen of Heaven; let us have a Mary with — yes! — "strong muscles and a merciful heart." Let us have a Mary who wears her crown at a jaunty angle on her head and snaps her fingers, so, at the things that frighten us. Let us have a Mary who hums a lively, finger-snapping rendition of an old standard: "Hail, Holy Queen, enthroned above, / Oh, Mah-ree-ah!" Clapping her hands, kicking her splendid legs as she swings on the crescent moon, Mary, Queen of Heaven, looks at each one of us like she just spotted an old buddy. Yes! Let it be.

Mary gets a kick out of being Queen of Heaven. She has strong muscles and a merciful heart. We take the whole business in such a deep and solemn fashion, but Mary tips her crown on her head at a jaunty angle, laughs with joy, and cries out with a voice that shakes the stars and makes them sparkle even brighter in the night sky: Rejoice! she cries. The Queen of Heaven cries, Rejoice!

You find darkness in your life? asks Mary, Queen of Heaven. You find darkness in your life? Listen to me, for I have strong muscles and a merciful heart. Listen to me. There is only one answer for the darkness in your life, only one reliable Light: the Lord, the Christ, my Jesus whose muscles are stronger than mine and from whom I get all the mercy in my heart. Oh yes, all the mercy in my heart.

Mary is Queen of Heaven, the playful Queen of Heaven with her crown at a jaunty angle, sitting on the crescent moon, kicking her splendid legs, looking down with love and delight at every hair on our heads. Into the closet goes the serene Madonna, eyes downcast, dressed in a flowing gown, trimmed in gold, crown perched perfectly above a serene, flawless face. Her perfectly prayerful, slender hands never changed a diaper, scrubbed a floor, or washed the dishes. Into the closet, Lady. You're harmless, we suppose, but you're not much fun, so into the closet.

Rebecca Wells' Mary gets a kick out of being Queen of Heaven: "From her perch on the crescent of the harvest moon, the Holy Lady looked down and smiled at her imperfect children."

She does, you know. She does.

Holy Mary, Queen of Heaven, pray that I may seek the true Light. Amen.

Our Lady of the Rosary (October 7)

The tradition that Mary gave the [rosary] beads to St. Dominic in the thirteenth century...is very strong in Roman Catholic circles and was not questioned for hundreds of years. The basic facts, however, give no justification to such a tradition....

Even if the tradition is not factually true, it is still perfectly valid to keep as legend. It is historical fact that St. Dominic had great devotion to our Lady.... All of the truths of which the rosary speaks are compressed and made concrete for us in the story of Mary's appearance to Dominic.... It must be remembered, however, that one should understand the vision as legend and not confuse it with historical fact.

— Richard Gribble, C.S.C.,
*The History and Devotion
of the Rosary* (1992)

Sing, O legend, sing a song of the Lady of Heaven, strong muscles and a merciful heart, who gave the rosary to Saint Dominic. Sing a song of Dominic at prayer, or Dominic preparing to preach the gospel along the dusty roads and in the tumbled-together villages of thirteenth-century Italy, or Spain, or France. Better yet, sing of Dominic slapping together a ham and swiss on rye, with mustard and mayo, an evening snack.

Sing, O legend, sing. Dominic glances up, out of his window, and there is the Lady, strong and merciful, sitting on the crescent moon, kicking her splendid legs like the moon is her swing, and the sky her front porch. She waves at Dominic like she just spied an old buddy. She did, in fact. She did. Dominic smiles and waves back. Old buddy. The Holy Lady waves and smiles, then she pushes a hand into the pocket of her glowing golden bib overalls — "Oshkosh, b'gosh" — and pulls out the plainest, plainest rosary beads, drab brown beads strung along a dull little chain, with a tarnished metal crucifix.

The Holy Lady tosses the plain rosary beads to Dominic who catches them with one hand while he licks mustard off the finger-tips of his other hand. What's this? he wonders. The Holy Lady, strong muscles and a merciful heart, must have something in mind. Dominic glances up. The Holy Lady waves. Dominic looks at the beads in his hand. Ah, he thinks. Of course. The beads are for keeping track of the days of the liturgical calendar. Hence the crucifix. No, that can't be it. The string of beads is for praying! That's it. Each bead is for a prayer. The Holy Lady gave him the beads, so each bead should be for an Ave Maria. The single bead between each string of ten beads can be for a Pater Noster. Aves and Paters. Good idea. Each series of ten beads could be matched with an event from the Gospels. That Dominic, he's a clever one, no dullard. He can do more than slap together a ham and swiss on rye. Dominic looks back at the Holy Lady and waves his thanks. She waves back again, her golden bib overalls — "Oshkosh, b'gosh" — sparkling in the moonlight. Old buddy.

Sing, O legend, sing of Dominic on the dusty roads of Italy, or France, or Spain, giving away strings of drab brown beads to the people he meets, recommending the new prayer method to his fellow friars, to scholars, to Francis of Assisi when they meet, whopping each other on the back. Old buddy. The idea catches on. Something about it makes it catch on with common people, monks and nuns, denizens of the universities. The rosary catches on. It's a simple way of prayer, but something about it is deep, too, profound. You could pray this way of prayer when you're feeling good or when you're feeling bad. You could pray this rosary kind of prayer just about any time, any place. When you can't pray any other kind of prayer you could pray this rosary. So it catches on.

Down through the centuries the rosary catches on and hangs on. It's a winner. Something about it makes it a winner over the long, long haul, down through the centuries. Something about the rosary is strong and merciful. Sing, O legend, sing.

Holy Mary, pray for me that I may often pray the rosary for others. Amen.

Presentation of the Virgin Mary
(November 21)

"And the child was two years old, and Joachim said, 'Let us take her up to the Temple of the Lord, that we may pay the vow that we have vowed....' And Anne said, 'Let us wait for the third year, in order that the child may not seek for father or mother.' And Joachim said, 'Let us so wait.' And the child was three years old...and they went up into the Temple of the Lord, and the priest received her and kissed her and blessed her, saying, 'The Lord has magnified thy name in all generations. In thee, on the last of the days, the Lord will manifest His redemption to the sons of Israel.' And he set her down upon the third step of the altar, and the Lord God sent grace upon her; and she danced with her feet and all the house of Israel loved her. And her parents went down marveling, and praising the Lord God because the child had not turned back. And Mary was in the Temple of the Lord as if she were a dove that dwelt there...."

— from the *Protoevangelium of James*

Oh, if you can imagine. If you can imagine a feast of Mary to mark an event that almost certainly never happened. A feast of Mary, smack-dab in the official liturgical calendar of the church, a celebration of an event that happened only in some pious writer's imagination. Not historically. It's enough to make you laugh right out loud, it is such a delightful, such a wonderful fact. The church hedges its bets, however, because no place in the liturgy for this day will you find mention of this almost certainly fictional event. It's quietly hilarious, that's what it is.

The story, as fictional as *Rebecca of Sunnybrook Farm,* from the apocryphal Gospel of James, is a pious delight. The second-century author knew who Mary was, of course; the author knew who Mary became, *Theotokos,* Mother of God, so it was easy enough to project back onto the childhood of Mary marvelous events foreshadowing her future role as mother of the Messiah. Never happened, but true all the same. This story was the author's way to say that even as a young child Mary had an amazing future ahead of her. Even as a young child she was who she would become.

While the story is fictional, it may not be completely out of touch with possibilities. On rare occasions even very young children show themselves to have remarkable gifts. Wolfgang Amadeus Mozart, in the mid-eighteenth century, is one of the best known. It is historical fact that he was a musical genius at a very young age. As a three-year-old, Wolfgang exhibited remarkable musical talent. At age four he learned to play the harpsichord and began composing music. When he was six years old he played for the empress of Austria at her court in Vienna. If you can imagine.

Mozart was a musical prodigy, so is it not remotely possible that Mary could have been a spiritual prodigy? It's possible. Even if the story from the Gospel of James, that pious piece of literary cotton candy, is fictional, still it could be true. Perhaps when the church decided — rather late in history, it's true, 1585 — to give the Presentation of Mary a place in the liturgical calendar there was more concern for truth than for historical fact, more concern for poetry than for science.

Why not? we may ask. Why not? Even if the story is not historical as we judge such matters today, it is truthful and delightful, and is it not good to celebrate truth and delight when it comes to Mary? Is it not good?

In the end, of course, we are left with the story and its various parts, each detail worth examining, even worth giggling over. In the end, perhaps we are left with that one sparkling phrase: "and the Lord God sent grace upon her; and she danced with her feet and all the house of Israel loved her."

Do we not find truth and delight even in these few words?

Holy Mary, pray that I may learn to imitate your joy and faith. Amen.

The Immaculate Conception
(December 8)

The "splendor of an entirely unique holiness" by which Mary is "enriched from the first instant of her conception" comes wholly from Christ: she is "redeemed, in a more exalted fashion, by reason of the merits of her Son." The Father blessed Mary more than any other created person "in Christ with every spiritual blessing in the heavenly places" and chose her "in Christ before the foundation of the world, to be holy and blameless before him in love."

— *Catechism of the Catholic Church*, no. 492

The idea of "immaculate conception," my oh my. It has become fodder for standup comedians. Even many Catholics think it refers to Jesus' conception by the Holy Spirit. Not so, not so, not so. Let the truth be told, may it circulate far and wide, wide and far.

The Feast of the Immaculate Conception is a Marian celebration, oh yes. It is the liturgical celebration of Mary's freedom from the effects of Original Sin from the moment of her conception, which took place in the usual manner through the pleasure of her parents. Let us not blush about this. Heavens above. The Immaculate Conception is a spiritual, not a biological, concept. Let us be done with the snickering humor of jokes about "immaculate conception." Please.

Pope Pius IX, in the mid-1800s, consulted with 603 bishops, asking if he should declare the Immaculate Conception a dogma of faith. Fifty-six thought about it, frowned, and believed it would not be a good idea. The rest approved. Long-held tradition and the great majority of the bishops on his side, the Pope proclaimed the dogma of the Immaculate Conception on December 8, 1854. Spake he in a voice quiet yet firm:

> The most Blessed Virgin Mary was, from the first moment of her conception, by a singular grace and privilege of almighty God and by virtue of the merits of Jesus Christ, Savior of the human race, preserved immune from all stain of original sin.

Protestants and Orthodox Christians had fits, and they had some great 12th and 13th century theologian-saints on their side, such as Anselm, Bernard, and Thomas Aquinas. But there you are. Other theologians and fathers of the church expressed approval of the Immaculate Conception as an act of the redemptive grace of Christ. In the 12th century, for example, the great theologian Duns Scotus approved, and Eadmer of Canterbury wrote:

> All men sinned in Adam (Romans 5:12). This statement is certainly true and I declare it would be impious to deny it. But when I consider the eminence of God's grace in you [Mary], I find that in a truly remarkable way you were placed not among but above all other creatures; hence I conclude that in your conception you were not bound by the law of nature like others, but by the extraordinary power and operation of divinity, in a way transcending human reason, you were preserved from all taint of sin.

The idea of the Immaculate Conception began to sing, sing in the hearts of Christians from the earliest days of the Christian community. Recall the angel's first words to Mary in the Gospel of Luke: "Greetings, favored one! The Lord is with you" (1:28). Remember, in the same Gospel, Elizabeth's "loud cry" to Mary: "Blessed are you among women, and blessed is the fruit of your womb" (1:42).

Now comes that most important of all theological questions. Here it is: *So what?* Here is so what: The dogma of the Immaculate Conception of Mary sings to us that the saving power of Christ knows no limits, not even the limits of time and space. The grace of Christ's redemption was retroactive in the life and being of Mary, his mother. The Immaculate Conception reminds us, in the words of theologian Elizabeth Johnson, that for all of us "grace is more original than sin."

Holy Mary, pray for me that I may abandon myself to God's love. Amen.

Our Lady of Guadalupe (December 12)

Our Lady of Guadalupe, mystical rose, intercede for Holy Church, protect the Holy Father, help all who turn to you in their necessities, and, since you are the ever Virgin Mary and Mother of the True God, obtain for us from your most holy Son, the grace of keeping our faith, sweet hope in the midst of the trials of life, burn-

ing charity, and the precious gift of final perseverance.
Amen.

— A Prayer to Our Lady of Guadalupe

Who does not know the story, the dazzling, holy story of
the Aztec peasant and the marvelous lady who appeared to
him on a hill called Tepeyac, outside of Mexico City? Tepeyac, site of an ancient temple of Tonantzin, Aztec virgin
mother of the old Aztec gods. On the morning of December 9, 1531, Juan Diego was minding his own business, on
his way to church. Walking, walking, trudging along, on
his way to the holy Mass, Juan Diego must cross the hill
called Tepeyac to get to the mission church. Walking along,
walking, walking, Juan Diego wears a tilma against the chill
morning air.

Suddenly Juan Diego sees a beautiful lady who looks to
be with child. She speaks to him in his own Aztec language:
"Know and understand that I am the ever-virgin Holy Mary,
mother of the true God, from whom one lives; the Creator,
the Lord of Near and Togetherness, the Lord of Heaven and
Earth." Later, in another appearance to Juan Diego's uncle,
the lady calls herself Our Lady of Guadalupe.

The holy lady gives Juan Diego a message for the bishop:
"I ardently desire that a shrine may be built on this site, so
that in it I can give all my love, compassion, help and protection; for I am your most holy mother, ready to hear all
your laments and to alleviate all your miseries, pains and
sufferings."

As a sign of authenticity for the bishop, the lady causes
roses to bloom on Tepeyac in December. She directs Juan
Diego to fill his tilma with roses for the bishop. When the

peasant opens his tilma for the bishop, out tumble the flowers and on his tilma is a picture of the lady herself. The picture is of a young Aztec woman, apparently pregnant. Later, some pious artist will add a gold border and gold stars to the lady's garments, plus a sunburst background, and under her feet a cherub angel and a crescent moon. These pious added touches will show signs of deterioration, but the original image will not. Powerful magnification will reveal in the eyes of the lady images of the first people who saw her picture on the tilma. The garment is woven from cactus material that normally would fall apart in twenty years. This miraculous garment remains intact more than four hundred years later, displayed in the cathedral of Our Lady of Guadalupe, in Mexico City.

Lady of Guadalupe, what is your message for us today? You came to people whom the Spanish had subdued. You appeared as a poor Aztec woman, not as someone foreign, someone identified with the conquering Spanish culture. Thus you gave back to millions of Aztec Indian people their dignity. Your desire to give "love, compassion, help and protection" clashed with the image of God taught by the Spanish. Their God inspired courage, but he was also a judge who condemned sinners to everlasting hell. The God of the Spanish showed little understanding or compassion.

Juan Diego was beatified — which makes him Blessed Juan Diego, one step from canonized sainthood — in 1990, by Pope John Paul II. Blessed Juan Diego, pray for us. Mary appeared to Juan Diego, the simple Aztec peasant, not to the bishop, not to some other official church personage. Mary appeared four times to Juan Diego, she spoke to him, she filled his tilma with roses in December, and she placed her picture on his tilma to last, a sign of the lasting love and compassion of God.

Mary, the Lady of Guadalupe, is a just romantic. She sings and sings across the centuries her song of justice and love. The gospel should be carried to people in the clothing of their own culture, she sings. The gospel is no excuse to force foreign cultures on people. Sing, Lady of Guadalupe, sing. Remind us, again and again, that our God is "the Lord of Near and Togetherness." When, again and again, we fashion for ourselves a God — forbidding, cold, distant and ready to condemn for the slightest reason — call us back to the true God. Call us back to the true God of love, compassion, and mercy. Call us back, Lady of Guadalupe, call us back to the God of Near and Togetherness.

Our Lady of Guadalupe, pray for us.

MARIAN APPARITIONS

(These are private revalations judged legitimate by Church authorities, but Catholics are neither required to believe in the apparitions themselves, nor are they required to believe in the validity of the revelations allegedly disclosed. It's up to you…)

Our Lady of Guadalupe

See pp. 76–79 above.

The Visions on the Rue du Bac

Mary the dawn, Christ the perfect Day;
Mary the gate, Christ the Heavenly Way!

Mary the root, Christ the Mystic Vine;
Mary the grape, Christ the Sacred Wine!

Mary the wheat, Christ the Living Bread;
Mary the stem, Christ the Rose blood-red!

Mary the font, Christ the Cleansing Flood;
Mary the cup, Christ the Saving Blood!

Mary the temple, Christ the temple's Lord;
Mary the shrine, Christ the God adored!

Mary the beacon, Christ the Haven's Rest;
Mary the mirror, Christ the Vision Blest!

Mary the mother, Christ the mother's Son
By all things blest while endless ages run. Amen.

— from the *Liturgy of the Hours*

Mary, you are so unpredictable. God, it seems, wants you to be unpredictable. The Creator of the Universe smiles and calls you to unpredictable love. Surprise them, Mother, instructs your divine son. Surprise them when they least expect it. Oh, yes, surprise them with love. And so she does, she does.

The Blessed Virgin Mary, young girl of Nazareth, mother of God's own Son, and mother to us all, delights in surprising us. How else are we to interpret her appearances to unsuspecting humans? What a surprise for Juan Diego. He never expected a beautiful lady on Tepeyac, the December roses he gathered into his tilma were a surprise, and the portrait of the beautiful lady on that same tilma was an even bigger surprise. You could have knocked him over with a chicken feather. He never expected to hear from the lady that our God is "the Lord of Near and Togetherness." Not in a million, million years.

Next, 300 years later — a mere flick of an eyelash — Mary appears to a nobody, an obscure French Sister of Charity of St. Vincent de Paul named Catherine Labouré. Catherine, Catherine, God whispered the name in Mary's ear. Pious enough, Catherine went about her prayers in her convent chapel on the Rue du Bac, in Paris. Saying her prayers, minding her business, pious enough but nothing mystical, saying her ordinary prayers in her ordinary way. But Mary is a surprising Mary with surprises up her sleeve.

Juan Diego was a 16th-century Aztec peasant crossing a hill, a hill with a past, near Mexico City. This is 19th-century Paris, and Sister Catherine is a 19th-century French nun, pious enough, saying her 19th-century prayers in a 19th-century French convent chapel. Surprising Mary appears to Sister Catherine in a surprising way, but still in a way that will make sense to a 19th-century French nun who is pious enough. Mary would never present herself to Catherine Labouré as the lady of Guadalupe, no. That would be *too* big a surprise. Surprising enough, she appears as a classic Madonna, an image from the cathedral of Notre Dame, perhaps, or Chartres. Catherine's surprising Mary stands, rather prim, on a half-globe. Rays of light stream from her fingers, quite a surprise. Words appear around her, another surprise, words floating in the air, words in French, *mais oui!* The words say this: *O Marie conçue sans péché priez pour nous qui avons recours à vous.* O Mary conceived without sin, pray for us who have recourse to thee. *Mais oui!*

Well, you can imagine. Sister Catherine was surprised by Mary, surprising Mary. But she was not finished, surprising Mary. No. Catherine also saw a cross in her vision with the initial M — which stands for "Mary" in both French and English, of course — plus the heart of Jesus with a garland of thorns and the heart of Mary pierced by a sword, surrounded by twelve stars. Now all this was definitely, without question, 19th-century French, which means that it may not ring our chimes completely, we North Americans on the verge of the twenty-first century. So it goes.

Next, Sister Catherine, pious enough, heard a voice — not with her ears did she hear this voice, not with her ears but with her heart. Ordinarily, it would be difficult to believe that such a voice was real. It would be too easy to conclude that it was just her imagination, pious enough, running away with her. But not this time. She saw Mary with her eyes, a rather sophisticated Mary surrounded by words and symbols, so what were some words spoken in her heart compared to that?

Catherine "heard" the Blessed Virgin instruct her to have a medal struck that would represent — after a fashion —

what Catherine had seen in her vision. All who wore this medal with devotion, pious enough, would receive special gifts of God's own life — grace upon grace — through Mary's prayers on their behalf. Mercy.

Similar visions followed the first one until September, 1831, when Catherine gave the Archbishop of Paris, pious enough, an earful. The Archbishop thought about it long and hard, gave his permission for medals to be struck, and the rest is *histoire*. The "Miraculous Medal" became enormously popular, a help to many, pious enough, who would stay close to Christ and to his Blessed Mother. Does this particular form of devotion to Mary have a future? We, pious enough, can only wait and see, wait and see....

Holy Mary, conceived free from sin, pray for us, pray for us. Amen.

Our Lady of La Salette

Mary, the mother of Jesus, has played a consistent role in the spirituality of Catholic Christians of the East and West. Devotion to her has taken many different shapes through the ages, and the image of Mary has entered deeply into the Catholic imagination.

— *The New Dictionary of Catholic Spirituality,* Michael Downey, Editor

Thirteen years after her appearances to Sister Catherine on the Rue du Bac, in Paris, Mary appeared again in France. On

September 19, 1846, two children, Melanie Mathieu-Calvat and Maximin Giraud, were minding their own business, and their business was to keep an eye on some cattle. Their business was to keep an eye on a few cattle on a high mountain some miles from La Salette-Fallavaux. The cattle minded their business, too. The business of the cattle was to graze, moo when the bovine spirit prompted them to moo, and wander aimlessly as the sweet grasses bid them do so. Good grass here, good grass here, good grass over there. Moo, munch, munch, moo.

Melanie and Maximin reported that the Blessed Virgin appeared to them once. The children said that the Virgin spoke to them. There was no report that the Virgin spoke to the cattle, but neither is there a report that the cattle ran off in all directions, spooked. The cattle remained at peace as the Virgin spoke to Melanie and Maximin. This was none of the cattle's business, their business was to graze on the sweet mountain grasses and moo when the bovine spirit prompted them to moo. If they saw the Virgin, the cattle remained at peace and went about their business: munch, moo, munch, moo, moo.

Melanie and Maximin reported that as the Virgin spoke to them she wept. She spoke to the children in French, of course, but her tears were the tears of all humankind. The Virgin wept as she spoke, and the children were touched by her tears. The Virgin lamented the widespread lack of faith among the people. Then, how like a mother, she wept at the widespread use of foul language, four-letter words. How like a mother.

Then the Virgin wept because so many people were doing hard manual work on Sundays, the Lord's day. How quaint,

we may think. How utterly quaint, for we have lost a sense
of time moving in sacred cycles, of a need for Sunday to be
"a day of rest." Had we been there, with the two children
in 1846, with the cattle, we could have said to the Virgin,
"You ain't seen nothin' yet." In our time most people have
no choice in the matter. For many Sunday is a day away from
the job, for many it is not. Even if Sunday is a day away from
the job, it is a day of much activity. O Virgin Mother of La
Salette, in 1846, you ain't seen nothin' yet.

The Virgin explained to the children that if people did
not repent, turn over a new leaf, she would allow the judg-
ment of Jesus to roll down on a sinful world. Oh, my. This
is the part that perplexes us, that seems theologically sus-
pect, even. Mary controlling Jesus? This is not the way the
Christian cookie crumbles. Such a Jesus, and such a Mary,
do not set well with the Jesus and Mary we find elsewhere.
The Gospels, for example. In official church doctrines, for
example. In the mysteries of the rosary, for example. At
Guadalupe, for example. On the Rue du Bac, for example. Oh, my. Perhaps Melanie and Maximin did allow their
imaginations to run away with them when they got to this
part....

All the same, in the valley of the mountain where the children said the Virgin appeared, a spring began to flow, a sign
of mercy, love, compassion, and life. A spring began to flow,
and miraculous cures were associated with water from the
spring. Five years after the children reported their vision,
the bishop of Grenoble declared the legitimacy of the apparition. The bishop announced that as far as the Church
was concerned it was fine for people to pray to Our Lady of

La Salette. Everything was on the up-and-up, as far as the Church was concerned.

Our Lady of La Salette, pray for us, pray for us. Amen.

Our Lady of Lourdes

Today Lourdes is the shrine and center of pilgrimage with the widest international appeal. The apparitions are well documented. It has been the place where many miraculous cures have occurred. Popular piety and the liturgy are beautifully combined at Lourdes, which has inspired many people to devote themselves to the care of others. Mary and the Eucharist is a theme particularly evoked there.

—*Madonna: Mary in the Catholic Tradition,*
by Frederick M. Jelly, O.P. (1986)

The Mary of apparitions has surprises in store, surprises up her sleeve, surprises, and none more spectacular and convincing than those in a cave, in a cliff, near a hick burg called Lourdes, in the Bigorre region of southwest France, on the northern slopes of the Pyrenees. The time was February 11, 1858, and it was as cold as a French well-digger's nose. Three young girls, dressed almost in rags, scrounged the countryside looking for firewood, anything they could take back to their poverty-stricken homes to burn for heat. Near a high rock cliff called Massabielle, one of the girls, fourteen-year-old Bernarde-Marie Soubirous—completely illiterate, starving, and sick — saw a "soft glow" in a hollowed out area of the cliff. She later reported that she had seen this "soft glow" in the same place twice before while searching for wood.

But this time Bernarde-Marie, known to history as Bernadette, saw in the "soft glow" a "beautiful girl." The beautiful girl beckoned to Bernadette but she was glued to the spot by sheer terror. If you can imagine. The two other girls — one of Bernadette's sisters and a friend, Jeanne Abadie — found their companion kneeling, immobile, staring up at the cave. They looked, squinting, shading their eyes, but they could see nothing. The two girls shook Bernadette out of her transfixed state, she told them what she had seen, and the two girls decided that they had a cracked nut on their hands.

Further visions followed, and the result for Bernadette was no end of trouble and grief. Trouble and grief, trouble and grief, no end of trouble and grief. Bernadette's mother throttled her, and the neighbors berated her for making up stories. The village priest refused to believe her. Bernadette and her two friends returned to Massabielle, this time with holy water, and when the beautiful girl appeared again Bernadette threw holy water at her, which caused the beautiful girl to smile. Well, you can imagine.... That was a good one on Mary, but she has a sense of humor.

Meantime, Jeanne Abadie had climbed up above the cliff and rolled a large rock over the cliff which landed near Bernadette. Perhaps Jeanne Abadie thought she could short-circuit the whole business with a large rock. But Bernadette was in a transfixed state, gazing at her vision of the beautiful girl, and she didn't so much as flinch when the rock hit the ground, whomp.

Bernadette saw the beautiful girl on many other occasions, but still she could not discover her name. Speaking the local Bigourdan patois, she simply called the beautiful girl, "*Aquero,*" meaning "that one." Before long so many people, hundreds then thousands, came to follow Bernadette to the Grotto that she had to be led there by an armed guard.

On either February 25 or 26, during that day's apparition, at the beautiful girl's instruction Bernadette began digging furiously in the dirt just inside the cave, and a spring came up out of the ground that eventually flowed into a nearby river, the Gave de Pau. By the next day the spring produced twenty-five thousand gallons of fresh, clear water every twenty-four hours. Within hours a blind man had washed his eyes in the water and regained his sight, and a woman with a paralyzed hand dipped it into the water and regained full use of her hand. Whoa.

Pandemonium broke out. Riots occurred. Bernadette finally got pushy with the beautiful girl and insisted that she tell her name. During the sixteenth apparition, on March 25, 1858, the beautiful girl laughed at Bernadette's pushiness and announced: "*Que soy era Immaculada Concepciou.*" I am the Immaculate Conception.

The dogma of the Immaculate Conception had been defined just four years before, but it is highly unlikely that Bernadette, an illiterate country bumpkin, could have heard this title for Mary anyplace before. Indeed, its meaning was explained to her again and again in the days to come, but it was a long time later, after she learned to read and write, before she grasped its full meaning. Right away and ever since, of course, sceptics have charged that Bernadette could have heard the phrase "Immaculate Conception" around town, at home, or someplace else.

Oh Mary, Bernadette's "beautiful girl," you are such a card. Did you choose the pious, the professionally holy, the movers and shakers of the world or the church, to show yourself to at the place that would become the world capital of Marian apparition sites? No, not ever. You singled out an illiterate nobody, an obscure country girl, a poor, ignorant, starving girl. We love it, Mary, we love it. You are such a card.

Our Lady of Lourdes, pray for us because we need it. Amen.

Our Lady of Fatima

O most holy Virgin Mary, Mother of God, I, although most unworthy of being your servant, yet moved by your wonderful mercy and by the desire to serve you, consecrate myself to your Immaculate Heart, and choose you today, in the presence of my Guardian Angel and the whole heavenly court, for my special Lady, Advocate, and Mother.

— from the *Act of Consecration to the Immaculate Heart of Mary*

Astonishments arrive one right after the other. Between May and October of 1917, Mary appeared six times to three Portuguese children, Lucia Santos and Francisco and Jacinta

Marto. The apparitions took place in Fatima, a village in mountainous central Portugal. Mary told the children that her Immaculate Heart would triumph. She asked that the faithful pray the rosary, wear the brown scapular of Mount Carmel (see pp. 57–60 above), and she asked that people make daily sacrifices to make up for sins that offended her Immaculate Heart. Mary also showed the children a terrifying vision of hell.

Mary told the three children that she came from heaven and asked them to return to the same place on the same day each month. The children followed Mary's instructions, and each time the message was basically the same. On October 13, during the sixth and last apparition, Mary told the children that she wanted a shrine built on the site of the apparitions to honor her as "the Lady of the Rosary." She asked that people pray the rosary every day. She foretold the end of World War I. At this time, over 700,000 people witnessed the so-called miracle of the dancing sun. A tremendous downpour of rain had been going on, but suddenly it ceased. The sun came out, began to "dance in the sky," then plunged toward earth. The frightened people cried out to God to save them, the sun returned to its place, and all the rain-drenched pilgrims were suddenly dry and comfortable.

In the course of the apparitions at Fatima, Mary revealed three secrets to Lucia, Francisco, and Jacinta. She said that Francisco and Jacinta would die young. The brother and sister did, in fact, die within three years during a flu epidemic in 1919 and 1920. Lucia became a Carmelite nun and lived to be very old. She prayed with Pope John Paul II at Fatima in 1991.

Mary told the children that Russia would spread errors all over the world but would eventually be converted and this would be followed by an era of peace. The Russian Revolution did, in fact, occur on November 7, 1917, mere weeks after the children reported this message, and events since the early 1990s may confirm the second part of this second message.

The third message from Fatima has never been made public, but by all accounts it was delivered to the Pope. In 1991, Vatican officials said that the third message has not been revealed in order to avoid stirring up religious sensationalism, and in 1996 they repeated this announcement. One can only believe that common sense has triumphed in the case of the third Fatima message.

Oh Mary, oh Mary, oh Mary. What are we to make of all this? Here we stand on the verge of a new century, in a world so old and so new, and we hear that nearly a century ago you showed three children a terrifying vision of hell, talked of dark sins offending your Immaculate Heart, left hints that horrible things might be in the offing, sent the sun spinning in the sky, and asked people to pray the rosary. And to top it all off, the church gives its official seal of approval to the whole enchilada. Oh Mary, oh Mary, oh Mary.

It's true. No one is required to believe in this or any other Marian apparition. It's true. For many people today Fatima, in particular, seems to nudge us into incredulity. The whole business seems so far removed from the Mary we find in the Gospel of Matthew, and the Mary we find in the Gospel of Luke. All the same, who is to say? You are an astonishing Mary, no question about that. Perhaps you are a Mary quite contrary. We would put you in a little box, have you all figured out, and insist that you never step outside the boundaries of our expectations. It's true. But perhaps you are a Mary quite contrary.... If so, Mary, if all that the children said you said is true, then what are we supposed to do with it today? Now, on the verge of a new century, what are we to do with it today? This is a prayer to your kindness, Mary of Fatima, a prayer to you as the young girl of Nazareth who said yes to an angel, who said yes to becoming the mother of the Messiah. What is the connection, Mary, between you at Fatima and you in the Gospels? Help us to see clearly, prayerfully....

Our Lady of Fatima, pray for us that we may have clarity of mind and heart on the verge of a new century. Amen.

MARIAN
PRAYERS

Prayers to Mary go back at least as far as the "Angelic Salutation," the words of the angel Gabriel to Mary in the Gospel of Luke (1:28), which scholars date to about 75 A.D. The prayer commonly called the Hail Mary, which begins with the angel's words, is probably the most popular prayer to Mary of all time. As columnist Dan Morris once remarked, the Hail Mary is an all-purpose prayer, one suitable for just about any situation. When your child is ill you can pray a Hail Mary. When you are grateful for a sunny spring day, you can pray a Hail Mary. If you are unemployed or just found a new job you can pray a Hail Mary.

As with all prayers to saints, prayers to Mary ask for her intercession, her prayers on our behalf; they are not prayers of worship or adoration. This collection of traditional Marian prayers should serve as a devotional resource, helping to keep alive prayers to Mary loved by countless generations, as well as a few of more modern origin. The author favors retention of an occasional, admittedly archaic, "thee," "thy," and "thou," in some prayers for the sake of the poetry; also in the belief that sometimes the language of prayer should be something other than pedestrian. Sometimes even in translation, prayers to Mary retain the Latin title in which they were first written.

Act of Consecration to the Immaculate Heart of Mary

O most holy Virgin Mary, Mother of God, I, although most unworthy of being thy servant, yet moved by thy wonderful mercy and by the desire to serve thee, consecrate myself to thy Immaculate Heart, and choose thee today, in the presence of my Guardian Angel and the whole heavenly court, for my special Lady, Advocate, and Mother. I firmly resolve that I will love and serve thee always, and do whatever I can to lead others to love and serve thee. I pray, Mother of God, and my most kind and amiable Mother, that you will receive me into the number of thy servants as thy servant and child forever. Purify more all my thoughts, words, and actions at every moment of my life, that every step and breath may be directed to the greater glory of God, and through thy most powerful intercession obtain for me that I may never more offend my beloved Jesus, that I may glorify him in thee, in the company of the Blessed Trinity, through eternity in Paradise. Amen.

The Angelus

The angel of the Lord declared unto Mary:
And she conceived by the Holy Spirit.

Hail Mary . . .

Behold the handmaid of the Lord:
Be it done unto me according to thy word.

Hail Mary . . .

And the Word was made flesh:
And dwelt among us.

Hair Mary . . .

Pray for us, O holy Mother of God:
That we may be made worthy of the promises of Christ.

Let us pray. Pour forth, we beg thee, O Lord, thy grace into
our hearts, that we to whom the incarnation of Christ, thy
Son, was made known by the message of an angel, may,
by his Passion and Cross, be brought to the glory of his
Resurrection. Through the same Christ, our Lord. Amen.

Ave Regina Coelorum

Hail, Queen of the heavens!
Hail, Empress of the angels!
Hail, Root of Jesse, gate of morn!
From thee the world's true Light was born.

Rejoice, glorious Virgin
Lovelier than all the other virgins in heaven.
You are fairer than all the fair,
Plead with Christ, our sins to spare.
Amen.

Consecration to Mary

I, _____, faithless sinner, renew and ratify today in thy hands the vows of my baptism; I renounce forever Satan, his pomps and works; and I give myself entirely to Jesus Christ, the Incarnate Wisdom, to carry my cross after him all the days of my life, and to be more faithful to him than I have ever been before.

In the presence of all the heavenly court I choose thee this day for my Mother and Mistress. I deliver and consecrate to thee, as your slave, my body and soul, my goods, both interior and exterior, and even the value of all my good actions, past, present, and future; leaving to thee the entire and full right of disposing of me, and all that belongs to me, without exception, according to thy good pleasure, for the greater glory of God, in time and eternity. Amen.

— Saint Louis Mary de Montfort (1673–1716)

Consecration of the World to Mary

Hail to thee, Mary, who art wholly united to the redeeming consecration of thy Son!

Mother of the Church, enlighten the people of God along the paths of faith, hope, and love. Help us to live in the truth of the consecration of Christ for the entire human family of the modern world.

In entrusting to thee, Mother, the world, all individuals and people, we also entrust to thee this very consecration of the world, placing it in thy motherly heart.

Immaculate Heart of Mary, help us to conquer the menace of evil, which so easily takes root in the hearts of people today, and whose immeasurable effects already weigh down upon our modern world and seem to block the path toward the future.

From famine and war, *deliver us.*

From nuclear war, from incalculable self-destruction, from every kind of war, *deliver us.*

From sins against human life from its very beginning, *deliver us.*

From hatred and from demeaning the dignity of the children of God, *deliver us.*

From every kind of injustice in the life of society, both national and international, *deliver us.*

From readiness to trample on the commandments of God, *deliver us.*

From attempts to stifle in human hearts the very truth of God, *deliver us.*

From the loss of awareness of good and evil, *deliver us.*

From sins against the Holy Spirit, *deliver us.*

Accept, O Mother, this cry with the sufferings of all individual human beings, laden with the sufferings of whole societies.

Help us, with the power of the Holy Spirit, to conquer all sin: individual sin and the "sin of the world," sin in all its manifestations. Let there be revealed once more in the history of the world the infinite saving power of the redemption: the power of merciful love. May it put a stop to evil. May it transform consciences. May thy Immaculate Heart reveal for all the light of hope.

—Pope John Paul II

Hail Mary

Hail Mary, full of grace. The Lord is with thee. Blessed art thou among women, and blessed is the fruit thy womb, Jesus. Holy Mary, Mother of God, pray for us sinners, now and at the hour of our death. Amen.

The Magnificat

My soul proclaims the greatness of the Lord,
my spirit rejoices in God my Savior
for he has looked with favor on his lowly servant.
From this day all generations will call me blessed
for the Almighty has done great things for me,
and holy is his Name.
He has mercy on those who fear him
in every generation.
He has shown the strength of his arm,
he has scattered the proud in their conceit.
He has cast down the mighty from their thrones,
and has lifted up the lowly.

He has filled the hungry with good things,
and the rich he has sent away empty.
He has come to the help of his servant Israel
for he has remembered his promise of mercy,
the promise he made to our fathers,
to Abraham and his children forever.

—Luke 1:46–55

Mary, Help of Those in Need

Holy Mary, help those in need, give strength to the weak, comfort the sorrowful, pray for God's people, assist the clergy, intercede for religious. May all who seek your help experience your unfailing protection. Amen.

Memorare

Remember, O most gracious Virgin Mary, that never was it known that anyone who fled to thy protection, implored thy help, or sought thy intercession was left unaided. Inspired by this confidence I fly unto thee O virgin of virgins, my Mother. To thee do I come, before thee I stand, sinful and sorrowful. O Mother of the Word Incarnate, despise not my petitions, but in thy mercy, hear and answer me. Amen.

—Saint Bernard of Clairvaux (1090–1153)

Morning Offering of the Apostleship of Mary

O Jesus, through the most pure heart of Mary, I offer thee all my prayers, works, joys and sufferings of this day for all the intentions of thy Divine Heart.

Our Holy Lady

Our holy Lady, glorious Mother of God, the Queen of Heaven and our struggling race, exalted high above angelic choirs, fill up the vessel of our hearts with grace. With wisdom's purest gold enrich our hearts, and make them strong, intrepid with thy might; bedeck them with thy precious virtues all, which gleam with shining jewels, dazzling bright. Blest Olive Tree, endued with fruit by God, pour out on us the balm of mercy's oil, that we may pardon find and reach our goal, in bliss forever, after trial and toil.

May Jesus Christ, your Son, this favor grant, for he set thee over angels hosts to reign, and crowned thee with a royal diadem, enthroned thee as the Queen of Heaven's domain. Amen.

— Saint Anthony of Padua (1195–1231)

Prayer to Mary for the Sick

Mary, Health of the Sick, be at the bedside of all the world's sick; of those who are unconscious and dying; of those who have begun their agony; of those who have abandoned all hope of a cure; of those who weep and cry out in pain; of those who cannot receive care because they have no money; of those who ought to be resting but are forced by poverty to work; of those who pass long nights sleeplessly; of those who seek vainly in their beds for a less painful position; of those who are tormented by the cares of a family in distress; of those who must renounce their most cherished plans for the future; of those, above all, who do not believe in a better life; of those who rebel and curse God; of those who do not know that Christ suffered like them and for them. Amen.

Regina Coeli

O Queen of Heaven rejoice;
   alleluia!
For he whom you merited to bear —
   alleluia!
Has risen as he said;
   alleluia!
Rejoice and be glad, O Virgin Mary;
   alleluia!
For the Lord has risen indeed;
   alleluia!

Let us pray:

God, you gave joy to the world through the Resurrection of thy Son, our Lord Jesus Christ. Grant that we may obtain, through his Virgin Mother, Mary, the joys of everlasting life. Through the same Christ our Lord. Amen.

Salve Regina

Hail, holy Queen, Mother of Mercy: Hail, our life, our sweetness and our hope. To thee do we cry, poor banished children of Eve. To thee do we send up our sighs, mourning and weeping in this vale of tears. Turn, then, most gracious advocate, thine eyes of mercy toward us; and after this, our exile, show unto us the blessed fruit of thy womb, Jesus. O clement, O loving, O sweet Virgin Mary.

Soul of Mary

Soul of Mary, sanctify me.
Heart of Mary, inflame me.
Hands of Mary, support me.
Feet of Mary, direct me.
Immaculate eyes of Mary, look upon me.
Lips of Mary, speak for me.
O Mary, hear me.

In the wound of the Heart of Jesus, hide me.
Let me never be separated from thee.
From my enemy defend me.
At the hour of my death call me,
and bid me come to your Immaculate Heart;
that thus I may come to the Heart of Jesus
and there with the saints praise thee
for all eternity. Amen.

Tota Pulchra Es

You are all beautiful, O Mary.
The original stain is not in thee.
You are the glory of Jerusalem,
The joy of Israel,
The great honor of our race,
The advocate of sinners.
Virgin most prudent, pray for us.
Intercede for us with our Lord Jesus Christ.
Amen.

Published by Resurrection Press

Other Titles by Mitch Finley

SEASON OF PROMISES
Praying Through Advent
with • Julian of Norwich • Thomas Merton • Thomas à Kempis
• Brother Lawrence • Caryll Houselander • Max Picard

"... full of inspiration and encouragement. In a season full of busyness which tends to starve the soul, this is a wonderful source of spiritual food." — JOYCE RUPP, O.S.M.

"The format of this book makes it delightfully available and fitting for the kind of busy lives we all lead...." — *Foundations*

1-878718-31-2   64 pp. $4.50 paper

CATHOLIC IS WONDERFUL!
How to Make the Most of It

"... it's a bouncy book when it comes to style. A bountiful book when it comes to content." — BILL GRIFFIN

"An itsy, bitsy, delightful volume on the Catholic Church ... sets down one of the finest, down-to-earth apologies for this mysterious thing known as 'being Catholic' I have ever read ... covers a lot of ground in a short time, and covers it well."
— DAN MORRIS, Catholic News Service Syndicated Columnist

1-878718-24-X   64 pp. $4.95 paper

SEASON OF NEW BEGINNINGS
Praying Through Lent
with • St. Augustine of Hippo • St. Teresa of Avila • John Henry Newman
• Dorothy Day • Vincent van Gogh • Flannery O'Connor

"Forget giving up candy for Lent. Stow the hair-shirt. Do something not constricting but convincing for Lent. Spend a few minutes every day singing along with Mitch, who's so light-hearted because he's so open hearted." — WILLIAM J. O'MALLEY, S.J.

1-878718-32-0   64 pp. $4.50 paper